69ers

A Novel About the 1969 Isle of Wight Festival of Music

by

Jon Blake

Grosvenor House
Publishing Limited

This book is published by
Grosvenor House Publishing Ltd
28-30 High Street, Guildford, Surrey, GU1 3HY.
www.grosvenorhousepublishing.co.uk

A CIP record for this book
is available from the British Library

ISBN 978-1-908105-65-3

Note to the reader: this novel originally began by quoting the first verse of The Ballad of John and Yoko. However, not wanting to kiss the ass of Sony/ATV Music Publishing nor pay them a penny for permission to use lyrics freely available all over the web, I trust to your own initiative in seeking them out for yourself.

ONE

The Ballad of John and Yoko was widely derided as the worst Beatles single to date, but Scott liked it. Not only did it feature two misunderstood outsiders against the system, but it also namechecked Scott's home town, unaccountably overlooked by composers despite its evident charisma as Britain's greatest passenger port, the city of Spitfires, first and only port of call of the Titanic, original departure point of the Pilgrim Fathers and unwitting harbour of the Black Death.

Yes, Southampton had a lot to answer for, besides the scowling handsome boy at Scott's side whose Dansette tinnily blared the Beatles' recent charttopper. Gerry was still fuming at Scott's idiocy, buying an old-fashioned canvas tent from the Army and Navy which weighed so much that Gerry was forced to carry both the haversacks, also canvas, frameless, and themselves backbreaking, all the more so because of the Philips EL3302 cassette tape recorder within, the key to Gerry's future, one of sufficient wealth and fame to net the girls of his frequent wet dreams.

Not that Scott saw it like that. He was merely concerned with posterity and spreading the messages which would surely change the world, just as the target of their flimsy microphone had predicted.

Meanwhile the old world stubbornly held out, in the shape of an endless stream of Minis, Cortinas, Imps and

Heralds cutting off the grammar school fugitives from the Red Funnel terminus and their ultimate destiny.

*   *   *

Scott roused himself from his well-worn armchair to kiss Angie goodbye. On her back was a well-stuffed rucksack and in her pocket a ticket to the V Festival. V, as any fool knew, stood for Virgin, the pseudohippy meganational which relieved the same fools of their air, train and culture fares, those fools including Scott who had spent the best part of a day on the phone being shunted around its various departments, none of which could seem to work out why his internet connection had been severed. The experience was not helped by the fact that Virgin's calming music of choice, the hits of Spandau Ballet, had exactly the opposite effect on Scott, whose spleen was still roused by these pouting poster boys of Thatcherism. In retrospect Scott could understand the scorn poured on the narcissism of the Ballad of John and Yoko, but at least there was some political purpose to it, no matter how hypocritical or misguided. What, on the other hand, could be said in defence of those kilted twaddlemerchants or their peers, except that their self regard was modest indeed compared to the rank tumour of self-reference that was to follow.

Still, this was allegedly the age of choice, when every other product was called Options, and Scott consoled himself with the fact that one click of a mouse could put him in the hands of another bunch of thieves and liars, to take advantage of the usual honeymoon period before they too ripped off their sheep's clothing and sank their teeth into his sadly limited wallet.

Scott had done his level best to alert Angie to the brutal realities underlying the bright lights, but the capitalists had learnt how to put on a good show, and the likes of Angie had learnt how to have a good time watching it. Festivals were a participation sport these days, full of community singing, flag waving, even mingling with the performers if you were lucky. Multiple stages, video screens, and to top it all, your own personal contribution to the great cause of the day, to be safely forgotten tomorrow. And who knows, the Red Arrows might even stage a fly-past, and we surely weren't far off the stage when battalians returning from fucking up some distant country might perform a homecoming parade.

Still, Angie did at least have her mum's groundedness, enough good sense to buy a decent tent and a pack of condoms, so that there was an even chance she'd stay both dry and free of the kind of STD which had fucked Scott's young kidneys and brought on a vicious circle of hypertension, congestive heart failure and oedema, sufficient, even when treated, to leave him with lifetime exhaustion and little remaining ambition beyond manning the desk at the International Community Centre.

Friends envied Scott's good fortune, landing a job which paid a living wage for doing virtually nothing, but a life of idleness could never suit such a restless soul. Despite his best intentions Scott had strayed into the dangerous waters of Twitter and Facebook, and it was through this blinkered self-exposure that he had unwittingly strayed into the path of a person inextricably linked to the memory of that historic summer, whose features, for good or bad, he would shortly face for the first time.

*　　　*　　　*

Scott leaned over the rail of the *Osborne Castle*, checking off the well-known landmarks of his childhood: the Vosper Thornycroft shipyards; Hythe Pier with its ancient train; Netley Castle, the flying boats, Fawley oil refinery, Calshot Spit lightship. It was impossible to travel down Southampton Water without being aware of how many old worlds rapidly aged: the flying boats, for example had had such a brief life, initiated by the likelihood of aircraft needing to land earlier than planned, a thought Scott preferred not to entertain, though he hardly needed to, having given airports a wide berth throughout his sixteen years.

The liners too had changed. Scott, who had memorised the funnel design of every major shipping fleet, still inwardly sighed at the abandonment of the Cunard tradition on the QE2. He'd watched the great new ship's maiden voyage from his usual vantage point in Mayflower Park, but preferred to turn his eyes to the Union-Castle liners faithfully queuing along the Western Docks, just as they had throughout his growing up, harbingers of a bigger world and a greater life than ever seen in the bungalow cul-de-sac he restlessly inhabited.

Travel to Cowes had changed as well. Scott's first loves, the makeshift car ferries Medina, Vecta and Balmoral, had been withdrawn, and purpose-built car ferries now ruled the waves. Hovercrafts and hydrofoils skimmed the tide. How appropriate it seemed that these icons of new technology were about to be swamped by the children of the new dawn.

It was Woodstock that lay behind Gerry and Scott's hastily-laid plans. Nothing had prepared the world for the monumental happening at Yasgur's farm, that massive and defiant demonstration of what freedom really looked like, how life could be lived to the full, and why a certain war was beneath contempt. Capitalism, which had created the teenager, stuffed his or her pockets with cash and encouraged him or her to seek out pleasure, had surely dug its own grave, and Richard Nixon was just as surely preparing to follow his astronauts out of orbit.

Gerry joined Scott at the rail, and despite himself Scott could not help experiencing a mild euphoria, having a companion for his adventure, a high-status male, furthermore, treated with respect by other boys at school, if not fondness. Scott had not always found it easy to find friends, especially after he fell foul of Ricardo Jennings, so Gerry's affiliation had been a surprise, his company an honour.

Scott breathed deep of the Solent air, solidarity and self-security.

"You're a funny looking fucker" said Gerry.

Scott made no reply. Like the beloved mum with whom he so struggled to communicate, he lacked the confidence to fight back, apart from those rare occasions when extreme stress lanced the boil of his pent-up rage.

"Your eyes are too close together" continued Gerry.

Scott kept his eyes averted.

"Your lips are like a woman's" continued Gerry.

Still Scott did not respond.

"Fight back" commanded Gerry.

"Haven't got the energy" mumbled Scott.

"You'll be no good at a three day shagfest" replied Gerry.

"I thought it was a pop festival" countered Scott.

"The music's just an excuse" responded Gerry.

But it was music that had united Gerry and Scott, in particular the desire to write a rock opera before they had mastered three chords. Oblivious to humiliation, they had performed their first efforts in the back bar at the *Royal George* on a Woolworth's chord organ and a mandolin. What they produced was barely music, but to their minds it was exactly its lack of attention to time, tune or structure which elevated it above the commercial crap that progressive rock was destined to supercede.

Like ten thousand others, Gerry and Scott felt uniquely worthy of the world's attention.

They did progress, however, inspired by a sense of mission which led them to mythologise every event in the band's evolution: a chance meeting with Tim the strumming telephone engineer became Stanley's encounter with Livingstone; a trip to Shaftesbury Road to buy amps and guitars became Moses's expedition to the Promised Land. Their choice of gear was less governed by its quality as its fitness for legend: a Baldwin Black Bison bass for Gerry, an Orange amp and speakers for Scott.

In their quest to create the new classic rock, Gerry and Scott made the classic mistakes of a virgin band, the first being to employ a drummer. It is a well-worn cliche that all drummers are mad, but like many cliches, it is founded in a germ of truth, related to the fact that drummers are people whose chosen means of self-expression is to hit something. The animal aggression of Stan Carey instantly transformed the band's sound, deleting all references to folk and inserting a new note of Gotterdammerung. Gerry and Scott were not at all opposed to this aspect of Stan's exhuberant percussion; it was when that exuberance involved the band's van or their own faces that their enthusiasm for Stan dwindled.

There is a time bomb ticking away beneath many bands, and Butterhorn was no exception. That time bomb is the drummer's own creative aspirations. Many months or even years may pass before he announces he has written a song which it is imperative the band perform. Of course, there is always the small possibility he may turn out to be a Robert Wyatt. But it is a very small possibility.

Stan Carey, it is fair to say, was no Robert Wyatt, even down to the rather miraculous fact he had not put himself, and the rest of the band, in a wheelchair. But besides owning the van, Stan owned the PA, at the controls of which he had installed his drowsily bored girlfriend, Jan, who loyally performed the Yoko role, seconding Stan's emergency resolution in support of his precious composition, and showing thitherto unseen energy in helping to pack up the gear after the inevitable row and split.

Tim was phlegmatic about it, but then Tim was almost always phlegmatic. As foreign to pretension as Gerry was to groundedness, Tim did his best with the rock operas but was far more at home with a classic blues or a concise slice of Cream. Tim was a dry character with a ready wit, a droopy moustache and an old Austin A35 which only sporadically committed itself to forward motion, its favoured action being an up-and-down clown-car bounce till whipped and cursed back into progress like a surly mule.

Scott liked Tim. Underlying his cynical wit Tim had a decent caring nature, and the best times in the band involved just the two of them and Tim's precious tape recorder, free from Gerry's overweening ego and Stan's furious impatience.

Tim was very nearly the last person Scott talked to, when Scott almost fell victim to that other great killer of rock musicians beside drink and drugs. The band had been on one of their gear-buying expeditions, resulting in a secondhand Farfisa organ for Scott, a quantum leap from the tinny buzzy toys he had thirtherto played. Back at the Victory Hall, having no plug, Scott taped the lead from his new organ to an extension wire. In the subsequent rehearsal, Scott was miraculously transformed into Keith Emerson, having just mastered the suspended 4th chord and now having an instrument which turned the band into a mini orchestra, in Scott's mind at least. After the practice, high as a kite, Scott unwound the plastic tape from the makeshift junction, pulled the wires apart and witnessed a blue arc of live electricity, inches from the shaking fingers that instantly dropped the two leads to the stage floor.

Calm as ever, Tim walked over to the side of the stage and took out the plug to which Scott had neglected to attend. "You were a nearly a pile of ashes that high" he remarked, indicating the height of the potential pile with typical concern for technical accuracy.

It was a moment Scott was never to forget, replaying his imaginary death many times, a fact of considerable relevance to the island adventure that was to follow.

Scott's close encounter with a river of electrons was not the only learning experience arising out of Butterhorn. Gigs were hard to come by, no offer turned down, including those from landlords and other patrons who completely failed to understand the implications of progressive rock. After Gerry had issued a press release announcing Butterhorn as the winners of a bogus poll for best live act at the Royal George, offers flooded in from the most unlikely venues, most sublimely untouched by the counterculture. Church youth clubs, dockers' institutes, rich kids' marquees, a virtual cross-section of southern England in 1969, yet all with the same curious proclivity for standing cross-armed and impassive in the face of future Britain.

The apogee of this run of gigs was a performance at Fawley Village Hall which was unique on many counts. Fawley was the site of allegedly the largest oil refinery in Europe, whose distinctive aroma, given the right wind conditions, perfumed the suburbs of Southampton and reminded those in the leafier suburbs that someone out there was doing the dirty work which helped to build their bijou semi.

Those hard workers also had children, and it was for these bored souls that a rare Saturday treat had been organised by an earnest youth worker, whose understanding of their needs unfortunately did not extend to an understanding of their taste in popular music.

Butterhorn set up in high spirits, Gerry experimenting with a pair of chiffon scarves tied to his wrists, Stan running through the difficult change to 6/8 time in the climactic movement to their rock opera *Shadows*, Tim attaching his prized cassette recorder to the hall's PA. Scott had thought it would help Stan to listen to their one-and-only live recording, made at their one-and-only successful gig, the week before at St Boniface Church Hall.

This gig wasn't looking so promising. No audience was in evidence. Then, on the stroke of 8, a lone skinhead walked into the hall, like a sentry ant, departing to exchange chemicals with his fellows.

The band began their set. The hall began to fill, quite quickly, with upwards of fifty youths of unenthusiastic demeanour. Evidently Ben Sherman shirts and Doc

Marten boots were very much *de rigeur* in Fawley, together with Alf Garnett braces and a choice of Levi jeans or the slightly smarter Sta-press trouser. In fact there was not a youth in the hall who did not share this uniform, apart from the four increasingly nervous young men on stage.

Hippy Dream, Butterhorn's opening crowd-pleaser, ended with deafening silence. A few skinheads sat on the edge of the stage, backs to the band. Not knowing what else to do, Butterhorn continued with the set, whereupon about twenty more skinheads joined their fellows in their strange silent protest, not only disconcerting but highly inconvenient for Gerry's balletic flourishes at key moments.

The first half of Butterhorn's set ended without a scintilla of applause or a single pair of eyes focussed in their direction. When Scott announced they were taking a break, the entire audience filed out. As there was no sign of their return when it was time for the second set, Stan's girlfriend was detailed to find out what exactly was going on.

Jan returned a few minutes later, wearing the same dowdy, vaguely drugged expression she adopted for every situation. "They're not coming back" she informed the band.

"Good" declared Gerry. "They can fuck off home and we can enjoy ourselves"

"They're not going home" replied Jan.

"Why's that?" asked Scott, adrenaline gently surging.

"They're waiting for you" said Jan.

"Did they bring their autograph books?" quipped Tim, but nobody laughed.

"They don't like your hankies, Gerry" said Jan.

Stan fumed. "I told you you looked like a twat!" he stormed.

Gerry was unapologetic. His chiffon scarves were a nod to the decorated hat of another sixteen-year-old, the preternaturally talented, effortlessly cool and femininely beautiful Andy Fraser of Free, the person Gerry most wanted to be and a secondary reason for his enthusiasm to get to the Isle of Wight.

Beneath his bravado, however, the little glands above Gerry's kidneys were, like Scott's, increasing his heart rate and diverting blood away from his brain and internal organs into his muscles, increasing his speed and strength, but probably not enough to either tackle or escape fifty booted skinheads.

Meanwhile those young warriors waited in sullen silence. Truth was, many were barely old enough for their muscles to have hardened, and few were blooded in battle. They'd been promised a Friday night dance with live band, and were entirely unprepared for a bunch of hippies to stray into their territory, or what appeared to be hippies to their unpractised eyes. But they understood enough of their chosen subculture to realise that these flouncing heavy rockers were the enemy, and that enemies were to be fought. The tribe's honour was at stake, and beyond that the very survival of white working class culture, or at least that brand of white working class culture which involved sharing the values and opinions of the biggest nobs in the land.

The alpha males had already staked out the territory. The band's van was round the back but the only exit was through the front doors. As *Technicolour Graveyard* blasted out from the hall, they guesstimated twenty-five to thirty minutes to armageddon.

The younger ones stared at their boots, nervously awaiting their opportunity to win their spurs.

Sadly, that opportunity was never to come. With *Technicolour Graveyard* still going strong there was a sudden roar of engine and the Butterhorn van burst round the corner, Stan's manic face mouthing urgent oaths. Stunned, the greener skinheads had no other thought than to fling themselves to safely. Not so Adey Tarrant, alpha of alphas, who threw himself onto the bonnet of the van and held on for grim death. Scott, who was sitting in the middle front seat, was never to forget the face that loomed so close to his own, the dull programmed eyes, the prematurely wrinkled forehead, the loose, meat-eating mouth. Through the seventies, the eighties, the nineties and the noughties, Scott never underestimated, possibly overestimated, the ability of our great leaders to rally its least educated citizens against the enemy within.

Adey Tarrant, however, was thrown off at the first corner, fracturing his left ankle on the kerb and duly waging a lifetime's war against all students, communists and longhairs until his premature death from AIDS in 1986.

The euphoria of the band's escape had faded long before they made their ritual stop at the KFC for supper. There was little doubt they had been over-optimistic about the prospects of recovering the gear too large to fit through the window of the gents' bogs, or Tim's treasured tape recorder, still faithfully broadcasting the only recording of what would turn out to be their sole successful gig.

The implosion of Butterhorn did not end the musical link between Scott and Gerry. Scott, who had learnt to hide his secret love of commercial music, especially those Motown songs whose yearning cries found an echo in his white Sotonian soul, was dragged along behind the caravan of Gerry's unstoppable passions, wherein every new purchase was a seismic event, every album cover pored over, deconstructed and committed to memory, every lyric analysed for hidden significance. Gerry's bedroom at the *Royal George*, when it wasn't in service as Gerry's shag nest, served as the crucible of culture. Tanked up on bottles of Stingo snaffled from the back bar, they would fall asleep under the dim red on-light of Gerry's Elizabethan stereo, listening to A Saucerful of Secrets, Days of Future Passed or Stonedhenge.

Gerry, it had to be said, was a freethinker. It took a freethinker to paper his walls with Baco Foil, advertise his services in the ladies bogs and fund his LP collection by trips onto the Royal George's roof to pilfer from his old man's mug of loose change through the window of his office. While Gerry lacked the comfort and stability of a happy family home, he was equally unconstrained by a happy family's expectations of normal behaviour. During their late night raps, when conversation strayed from music, Gerry loved to be frank about such subjects as his wanking habits, the boys he'd fancied at school, his expectation of early death and the nightmarish time he accidentally saw his estranged mother's cunt.

It was a one-sided conversation, as Scott was equally determined to keep such matters under wraps, especially the subject of his own virginity, an area Gerry probed mercilessly. Scott's lack of sexual experience was a great source of amusement to Gerry, who had particular fun exploiting Scott's ignorance about the 69 position. As the year was conveniently 1969 and proclamations from the underground were coming as thick and fast as papal encyclicals, Gerry managed to convince Scott that "The 69 Position" was a manifesto produced by Leary, Ginsberg and others holding that everybody should cease to cooperate with Babylon and build alternative circles which would in the fullness of time peacefully supercede the old world. Though Scott was not expecially gullible, Gerry was an exceptionally good liar, and under his influence a pissed-up Scott did ask a number of girls at the Friday disco what they thought of the position. He never received a reply, which only convinced him that Leary, Ginsberg etc had limited purchase on the UK proletariat.

Gerry had also got his dick out and chased Scott round the dark midnight bars once or twice, but it was only to enjoy Scott's horror. There was no attraction between them, although coincidentally they were both attracted to the same boy, Tim Doherty; one reason for their affinity to the art studios was that these afforded an excellent view over the volleyball court, where the small but perfectly-formed Tim's slim supple limbs and neat round bottom could regularly be witnessed. Typically Gerry had told Tim that he surely should have been cast as Romeo in Zeferelli's acclaimed film, while Scott's own passion remained so secret it had not even occurred to him that it signified bisexuality.

A love of one's fellow man, however, was hardly headline news in Southampton's most eminent school. But as the hair grew on the Beatles' faces, a new paranoia grew in the Isaac Watts staffroom. Hair was the thin end of the wedge; drugs were the chimera which threatened to destroy the reputation of the school. The Art department was the Trojan Horse which would carry the virus into the main body of the school, and anybody who painted strange psychedelic shapes (Gerry) or overexposed-photo-style portraits of Che Guevara (Scott) was treated with the utmost suspicion, thus conveneiently driving them further into the arms of the underground.

A copy of Oz left in the cloakrooms lit the blue touch paper for an inquisition which was worthy of Torquemada at his finest. The entire school was marched out onto the field for a bogus fire drill while teachers combed the cloakrooms like homicide detectives, rifling through the boys' coats and bags with feverish fingers. Whether the said teachers could have identified a tab of Mandrax or lump of red leb was a moot question, but disappointingly to Gerry none were found, and the search (which few had witnessed) was quickly airbrushed out of history.

Scott joined the rebels almost by accident. He'd realised early on in school life that he did not belong to the cognoscenti, that production line of Isaac Watts pupils issuing from the leafy suburbs where the exceptions were ones who failed 11-plus, not the ones who passed it. He found himself gravitating towards those pupils, primarily from the working and lower middle classes, who shared his healthy contempt for the great school traditions, who yawned through Orations and Declarations, who passed dirty notes during Founders and Benefactors, who skived the Beating of the Bounds. At the same time, however, Scott was bright enough to win the Parfitt Poetry Award, athletic enough to get four uppers at the Colts sports day, and sufficiently artistic to get his name in the Book of Digniora. So Scott was partially innoculated against the pure hatred others felt for the school.

It was the opening of Shades boutique which changed things. Though a basement near the Bargate, the

Checkpoint Cafe, was the surreptitious home of the experimental minority, Shades was the first outward manifestation of the counterculture in Southampton; a sunglassed wildhaired face sat atop its front window, provoking the ire of the chamber of trade who insisted in the removal of this blight from Above Bar – ironic, really, considering the devastation wreaked by postwar architects on the flattened centre of the city.

Another groundbreaking feature of Shades was the lighting, or lack of it. It was conveniently impossible to see the prices or any other details on the trendy but flimsy clothes. So when Scott first experienced its Middle Earth gloom in search of a new pair of school trousers, he was able to identify the desired twenty-six inch flares and double waist button but little else. Only on seeing his purchase in the cold fluorescent light of home did he discover that the trousers in question were not the regulation charcoal grey but a thoroughly unregulation dark blue.

Scott, typically, had lost the receipt, his mum was unsurprisingly unwilling to sponsor a second pair of trousers from her paltry wage packet, and Scott duly provoked the ire of teachers, yea, even unto the head teacher, while winning the admiration of the rebel faction, who typically sought out the palest greys it was possible to buy, but had not even countenanced anything as outlandish as blue.

Those blue flares were still in evidence on the deck of the Osborne Castle, much to Gerry's chagrin, who could not understand why Scott could possibly choose to wear school trousers to the most alternative event in Britain's history. Gerry took it as yet another sign of Scott's conformity, the same conformity which had led Scott to choose two more years of purgatory in order to get his A-levels and a place at university. Tension between the two had mounted since Gerry's unflagged announcement that he would not be returning to the Isaac Watts Grammar School for Boys after the summer.

Gerry's motivation for leaving school was unclear. He had the ability to get his A-levels, no doubt, even if one of his original choices, Art, was made more for reasons of style than talent. There was no family career waiting for him, not unless he wanted to skivvy in his dad's pub kitchen, which he certainly didn't. He didn't hang out with the casual drug experimenters at the Checkpoint Cafe, like half of that year's early leavers. In all probability Gerry was just fed up with school, with the petty restrictions, with being a grammar school boy when alternative lives were flowering all around the world.

Having made his decision, however, Gerry adopted an appropriate self-image which involved a thirtherto unseen attachment to the working class and contempt for students, including all those former friends destined for tertiary education.

In fact Scott was wearing his blue trousers for one simple reason: he had split his grey cotton jeans with the flare inserts, had nothing else remotely trendy, and could not afford four weeks' pocket money to buy a new pair. Besides, his decision to stay on did not represent a softening of his opinions on the school – far from it. Scott had been put under extreme pressure by the Head of Sixth Form not to take Art, and since being caught hiding in the dark room during assembly had been informed that his prospects of becoming a prefect were slight.

Nor was Scott without his doubts about staying on. No-one in his family had been to university and such progress did not seem inevitable. Since they had hatched the plan to make the bootleg LP, a whole associated fantasy had arisen around it, wherein Scott became a freelance journalist, touring the world in pursuit of interviews with reclusive musicians. So the journey down Southampton Water, rather than constituting a short story, might become the first chapter of a novel which would wrench the restless sixteen-year-old entirely away from his predicted direction.

Two

Maurice Moss looked up at the two refugees with a caustic smile. "Rayner and Roche!" he cried. "What are you doing here? The Spastics' Convention's down the road!"

Maurice put down his toolbag and approached the self-conscious pair. They were standing on a dirt road between two fields, outside what was to be number one gate, at present a half-built scaffolding tower dividing a perimeter fence on which Maurice had been rigging fluorescent lights. With a sudden bound, Maurice seized Scott in a neckhold and wrestled him to the ground.

"Get off, Moss!" cried Scott.

Maurice released him, pecking order established. "What's that round your neck?" he scoffed.

Scott self-consciously fingered the Peter Rabbit hankie fashioned as a neckerchief. "Haven't you heard, Moss?" he replied. "It's the new school tie".

"Don't call him Moss" snapped Gerry.

"He called us by our surnames" protested Scott.

"Have you got first names?" scoffed Maurice.

Scott scrutinised Maurice. He wore a pair of Lennon-type blue-lensed glasses and his lank blond hair hung down past his ears, almost covering his neck. "Are you wearing a wig?" he asked.

"Bollocks I am!" replied Maurice. "Go on, pull it"

Scott did not respond. Maurice was still remembered as one of the firsties who peopled Ackermann's wanking club, and though he had since proved himself not to be queer, the aura of untouchability remained.

"How d'you grow it so long?" asked Gerry.

"I'm just fertile" replied Maurice.

"It's no good having long hair and a miniature dick" quipped Gerry.

"It's that what you say when you look in the mirror?" asked Maurice.

"I haven't got long hair" replied Gerry.

Maurice turned to Scott. He could sense Scott's discomfort at the frank conversation. "By the way, Rayner" he enquired. "Got your first pube yet?"

"Very funny" replied Scott. The memory of being the last boy in class to reach puberty was still uncomfortably fresh.

"So what have we got to do?" asked Gerry.

"I don't know" replied Maurice. "What can you do?"

"You told us you could get us work!" said Gerry.

"I said I *might* be able to get you work" replied Maurice. This was not how Gerry remembered the conversation when Maurice visited the *Royal George* on the first weekend of the summer holidays. Maurice's uncle was a standfitter who was supplying the marquees for the upcoming pop festival. Maurice was going to work for him, and there would be tons more jobs going, including guaranteed jobs for Scott and Gerry if Gerry could persuade the bar staff of the *Royal George* to furnish Maurice with two pints of snakebite. The mere mention of Maurice's name, Gerry was assured, would then be the passport to employment on the festival site, and with it those vital backstage passes which would guarantee interviews with the stars and a perfect site for a bootleg recording.

Suddenly those interviews were looking downright unlikely.

"You never said *might*" said Gerry.

"Yeah, well, you should have come last week" replied Maurice.

"You said three days before" said Gerry.

"They changed the schedule" lied Maurice.

"*Scheisse!*" hissed Gerry. He placed his hands on his hips and stared blankly round at the fields busy with workers.

"Thing is" said Maurice, "most of the people here have got a skill"

"I've got skills" snapped Gerry.

"Such as?" asked Maurice.

"Loads of things" replied Gerry.

"Can you rig lights?" asked Maurice.

"I could learn" replied Gerry.

"They want workers, not apprentices" said Maurice.

"What are you doing, anyway?" asked Gerry.

"Working with the sparks" replied Maurice.

"I thought you were doing the tents" said Scott.

"Nah" replied Maurice. "The tents were on schedule, so Bill asked me to do this"

"Who's Bill?" asked Gerry.

"Bill!" replied Maurice. "Bill Foulk. The gaffer"

"Never heard of him" said Gerry.

"Bill's a great guy" remarked Maurice. "People think Ron and Ray pull the strings, but Bill's the man"

Scott, already weary from the journey, began to feel an additional weariness. Far from leaving the Isaac Watts Grammar School behind, here they were trapped on an island with one of its most tedious products.

Maurice had the whip hand and was determined to make the most of it.

"You could always ask Ron" suggested Maurice.

"Who the fuck's Ron?" replied Gerry, increasingly impatient.

"Ron" explained Maurice. "Ron Smith. Head of security"

"Security?" repeated Scott. "I'm not working for security!"

"Why not?" countered Maurice. " They're unskilled. Apart from the ones with dogs"

Scott was nonplussed. It had never occurred to him that uniformed men with alsatians would stalk this great festival of the free. Vaguely he wondered if Dylan knew about it.

"We've got to do something" said Gerry.

"I'm not being a policeman!" replied Scott.

"They're not police" scoffed Gerry.

"What are they doing here, anyway?" asked Scott.

Maurice pulled an idiot face. "What do you think they're doing?" he asked.

"I don't know" replied Scott.

"What, do you think we should just have a free-for-all?" asked Maurice.

"I thought it was a free-for-all" replied Scott.

"I think you'll find" replied Maurice, "it's twenty-five shillings for Saturday, two quid for Sunday, or two pound ten for the weekend"

"What, do you think they're going to let people just walk in?" asked Gerry, who, despite Maurice's betrayal, was starting to side with him.

"They don't need dogs" mumbled Scott.

"Tell you what, Scott" said Maurice. "You get a job with them, then you can persuade them to use lambs"

After the conversation with Maurice, Scott fell into a deep depression. Their plans to get work suddenly seemed ridiculous, they had no fallback, and Gerry's frustrated sniping as they explored the site made him insufferable company. Through Scott's dismal perspective, the supposed field of dreams looked more like an internment camp, already policed, as Maurice had promised, by a security force who restricted the schoolboys to a mere glimpse of the half-built stage where the historical event was to take place. This stage, with its mock classical pediment, was one frame in a seamless advert for cold scaffolding. The perimeter fences were supported by it, the entry towers built of it, the PA rig, the lighting tower, the temporary shops. Had Scott and Gerry spent as much time mastering joint-pins and swivel couplers as they had spent declining *agricola* and *puella,* their fortune would have been made. But then the whole point of grammar school education was to steer the likes of Gerry and Scott away from such a fate.

Even the electric supply depended on scaffolding poles, standing like sentries around the perimeter, catenaries hanging in sinister arcs between them, onto which were taped the cables that would bring juice to every corner of the site, cables that dipped to kiss the top edge of the perimeter fence every few sections in order to service a tenuously mounted fluorescent. With life, as Scott knew all too well, came danger. He did not fancy working with the electricians, but nor did he fancy scaling heights to work with the tent erectors, or undergoing cross-examination working with anybody.

But what an enterprise it was. And happening on the Isle of Wight! It barely seemed possible. Surely it was some kind of wind-up to site a drug-fuelled free-love music festival in the constituency of Mark Woodnutt MP, stalwart of the Monday Club, hanging enthusiast and Enoch Powell sympathiser. The island was the retirement home of choice for every other admiral and colonel in the land, a place where change happened as gently as the camber of Ryde Sands, affording nothing but shallow warm pools, not deep enough in which to swim, but neither deep enough in which to drown. Sure, the island had its Blackgang whale, its red squirrels, its Godshill water 'otter. But it did not do mindfuck psychedelia, unless you counted those test-tubes of coloured sands from Alum Bay, and what a disappointment that place proved to be, its beach no more kaleidoscopic than Sandown's.

Not that the Isle of Wight was completely free of the little green shoots of counterculture, a fact best summed up in the famous summary of the island's contradictions: Needles you couldn't thread, Ryde where you walked, Cowes you couldn't milk, and Lake where there was no water but paradoxically a series of progressive rock gigs featuring some of the biggest rising stars in the UK. Scott knew this because Butterhorn aspired to be one of these rising stars, failed to get the gig, and reached the inevitable conclusion that, while the island was beginning to rock, it was not yet ready for the vanguard.

Scott had actually been to one gig on the island, two years before, on a field, in a tent, and for him at least it had been a life-changing experience. Every two years the island held an industries fair which was a magnet for Scott's dad's tills and bacon slicers. Scott loved to wander around the various stalls, the fluffy toy makers and the rare jams, the sizzling rills of frying doughnuts, the gravel-voiced salesman with his magic cleaning potions. There was always an air display or a special feature such as James Bond's car from Thunderball, and in the evening one marquee was given over to live music and dancing. Inside that marquee, while the summer of love exploded half way across the world, a prepubescent Scott sat transfixed by the experience of a live steel band, more excited, if truth be told, than he ever was to be by any progressive rock gig on the mainland. The sight and sound of these vital men made him feel so inconsolably white, like a little soft pupa, that his petty half-life hardly seemed worth living.

It was this vision, of the pale pettiness of his existence, which drove Scott to the island this August bank holiday. Yes, he was going along with Gerry's plan to make a bootleg recording, but unlike Gerry, he was not motivated by what pleassures he might get, what money he might make, or what girls he might pull. He was motivated by another vision, the vision of what he might become, neither pale, nor petty, but something vital and powerful, something embodying the dignity of nature, something with a presence that others warmed to like a bonfire.

Now, gazing at the mud and metal infrastructure of the festival, Scott was already beginning to despair that he would ever break down his own barriers. It was such a step into the unknown, the only consolation being that everyone else was in the same boat: the contractors and their key workers ensconced in caravans backstage, the organisers and performers still safely inside bricks and mortar, the adventurers of various kinds hoping to prosper on the fringes of the action. No-one knew for sure what was about to take place.

The signs, however, were that big numbers were coming. Gerry and Scott, arriving several days early, had expected to pitch their tent in an empty field, but this was far from the case. Already the camp site to the east of the arena was dotted not only with tents but with makeshift dwellings, some of great ingenuity if questionable watertightness. Everyone knew that half a million had showed up at Woodstock, so who was to say the same might not happen at Wootton? No wonder so many residents had been up in arms when the entire population of the island was potentially to be outnumbered.

Two of the threats to island peace had already taken up residence a short distance from Scott and Gerry's tent, and when they returned from their halfhearted search for work late that afternoon, the new neighbours were pretty much unavoidable. One, a dark-haired lad about their age, squatted by a gaz stove, frowning hard as he stirred some concoction in a saucepan. The other, lanky and frizzy-haired, lounged back in a camping chair, coolly holding forth about something or other.

Scott, deep in a mindwash of negativity, headed for the mouth of his tent with blinkered purpose, but he was not about to escape so lightly.

"Hi!" said the dark-haired lad, with exaggerated friendliness. "Would you like some goulash?"

Neither Gerry nor Scott had ever sampled goulash, or such an opening gambit, which threw both of them onto the back foot.

"Just eaten, thanks" lied Gerry.

"It's vegetarian" added the dark-haired lad, as if this would cause a rapid reassessment.

"I'm allergic to vegetables" responded Gerry.

"Wow, really?" replied the dark-haired lad.

"He's taking the piss, Toby" drawled the frizzy one, with a calm authority that instantly intrigued Scott. The two young men had a demeanour which was quite foreign to him: the one called Toby, like them, had summer-holiday length hair, but also the beginnings of a respectable beard. He wore a mauve jumper full of holes, yet with neck and cuffs entirely unworn. He spoke as eagerly as a farmer's dog, but had a strange habit of absenting his eyes upwards beneath their lids, as if he really wanted to avoid eye-contact but could not be bothered to turn his head.

The frizzy one, on the other hand, was quite happy to meet their eyes, even though his chin was withdrawn as if expecting a punch. He was an odd-looking individual, with a narrow head, radar-dish ears and prominent nose and teeth. Nevertheless, his curiously still, reptile eyes and air of complete certainty afforded him an instant charisma.

Gerry asked his name.

"Clem" replied the frizzy lad.

"Clement" responded Toby, with a childish grin.

"Clem" repeated the frizzy lad, shooting Toby a dark look. "I was named after you-know-who"

Scott and Gerry didn't know who, but let it pass.

"Choose your spot" said Toby, gesturing around at the area in which Gerry and Scott might sit.

Gerry remained standing. Scott, still hoping to avoid any kind of challenging intercourse, sat down at a comfortable distance from the newcomers. Toby leaned towards him with a look of concern.

"Is that where you feel happy and strong?" he asked.

This wasn't a question Scott was expecting, nor had any prepared reply for. Clem came to his rescue. "Toby is a Castaneda devotee" he explained, with a wry smile..

"You really should keep an open mind about it, Clem" responded Toby.

"Tosh" said Clem.

Toby clearly wanted to respond to this, but had just tested the goulash, and according to his unbendable doctrine now had to chew this exactly thirty-five times before committing the food to his digestive system. It was a torturous business, Toby's agitated index finger indicating the urgency of the reply to be made.

"Clem can't adapt to the new way of thinking" he finally blurted.

"I thought it was an ancient way of thinking" countered Clem.

"New to us" replied Toby.

Clem addressed Scott. "Have you read *The Teachings of Don Juan*?" he asked.

"Byron?" asked Scott.

"Castaneda!" replied Clem, and for a moment he and Toby were united in laughter, tunnelling Scott straight back into the shell he was tentatively escaping. "I recommend it" he continued. "Funniest book I've ever read"

Toby chose not to take the bait, readdressing himself to the bubbling pan.

TOBY CAMPBELL'S VEGETARIAN GOULASH
1 cup aduki beans, soaked
1 onion, roughly chopped
1 beetroot, half-cooked, roughly chopped
2 sticks celery, diced
1 potato, sliced
Sprinkling of mixed herbs

Toby made no compromises as a cook. He took the view that the addition of stock cubes or other adulterants prevented the natural flavour of the pulses coming through; in the case of the aduki bean, a flavour remarkably similar to sausage, without the moral implications. Not everyone could appreciate that similarity, but then others' tastes were corrupted by Smiths crisps and Birdseye beefburgers.

Some of a cynical bent might have countered that Toby's own taste was corrupted by his moral imperatives, imperatives which crowded out any possibility of aesthetic awareness. After all, wasn't the whole point of a public school education to destroy normal human functions and reprogramme the individual as a servant of Empire? Even though, in the cases of Clem and Toby, Dulwich College had failed miserably to turn out pliant patriots, the two remained marked in every other way by their peculiar upbringing.

"How long does it take to cook?" asked Scott, grateful to find a subject about which he felt confident.

"About an hour" replied Toby.

"An hour?" echoed Scott. "Isn't that going to use up a lot of gas?"

A flicker of irritation passed over Toby's face. "It's nearly ready" he muttered.

Scott had never in his life tasted a meal as bad as Toby's goulash, yet he ate it in a mild euphoria. His earlier despair had evaporated after the first forkful with the sudden awareness that he was actually here, at Wootton Bridge, the most important place to be in the UK, maybe the world. He'd found two people the like of which he had never met, they had accepted him as a friend and offered him food. This, surely, was what they had come for.

"I can't believe we're going to see Dylan" he enthused.

"If he turns up" replied Clem.

"Why shouldn't he turn up?" asked Scott.

"He lives in Woodstock, and he never played there" replied Clem.

"He lives in Woodstock?" replied Scott. "I never knew that"

"They probably had the festival there just to piss him off" remarked Toby.

"Why should they want to do that?" scoffed Gerry. Unlike Scott, he was not warming to the new communal life.

"There are a lot of people who are frustrated that he hasn't played so long" opined Toby.

"That's up to him" said Gerry.

"I'm just saying, some people are frustrated" replied Toby, defensively.

Scott was beginning to wish he'd come without Gerry.

In his own element Gerry was full of swagger, but in this unknown environment his insecurities were making him an embarrassment.

"This will be his first gig in four years" Scott announced, hoping to derail the budding row.

"That's a common misconception" proclaimed Clem. "It's not his first gig since the accident"

We awaited further elucidation. "He played a Woody Guthrie memorial concert in January last year" continued Clem. "Two shows."

Gerry's first instinct was to dispute this, but like Scott, he had never met anybody their age who spoke in such a considered and authoritative manner, or in such a peculiar voice. Clem's voice was almost a gargle, as if he were being gently strangled, while his accent travelled from Hampstead to the East End and back again within the same sentence.

"If there was an accident, that is" added Clem.

"Oh, come on!" laughed Gerry.

"Dylan was never hospitalised" continued Clem. "His wife was the only witness"

"Why should he fake an accident?" scoffed Gerry.

"That's a good question" replied Clem.

"Answer it then" challenged Gerry.

"I can only speculate" replied Clem.

"Go on then, speculate" pressed Gerry.

"Well" replied Clem. "He never liked being regarded as the spokesman for the young generation…"

"Crap" said Gerry.

"…I think he wanted a complete break so he could remake himself" continued Clem.

"Absolute crap" said Gerry.

"Hey, come on…" intervened Toby.

"Anyone who thinks he faked that accident is off their fucking trolley" proclaimed Gerry.

"Clem's got a right to his opinion..." said Toby.

"I've seen the fucking bike!" snapped Gerry. "It was a fucking write-off!"

In the face of this outburst Clem sat very still, mildly stunned, weathering the storm, before recovering the offensive. "What make was it?" he asked.

"It was a fucking *write-off*!" repeated Gerry. "How could I see the fucking make?"

"Hey!" yelled a voice from nowhere.

The voice had an American accent and issued from an improvised canvas shelter, tucked into a hollow at the field's edge like a psychedelic dugout. Four figures sat there in a line, all long-haired, bearded, kitted out like well-worn nomads. They looked like some kind of chorus, there to comment on the main action, but when the speaker climbed out to make himself known, he did not look one bit a supporting player: tall and handsome in a sheepskin waistcoat and collarless shirt, he could have been a man of nature all his life, though the first summer of love had happened only two years earlier.

"Cool it, man" he said to Gerry, hands performing a damping down gesture. "We're here for peace"

Gerry was not used to anyone looking him in the eyes with neither adoration or aggression, and Joe really did have remarkable eyes himself, clear and easy and brown with black lines around the pupils. Such was his natural authority that Gerry's fury, which could simmer for hours, simply dissipated.

"Hey, you guys" continued the American, offering a hand all round. "My name's Joe"

Introductions ensued. Toby brimmed with excitement. "Where have you come from?" he asked.

"Woodstock" came the reply.

Toby's eyes opened wide. "Woodstock?" he exclaimed. "Wow, what was it like?"

"Well, man" replied Joe, wistfully. "You just had to be there"

Toby nodded emphatically, as if this reply had given him all the information he needed. Meanwhile Scott had resolved not to be overawed by the newcomer, but to slip into the conversation as easily as Joe had originated it.

"Have you ever been to the Isle of Wight before?" he asked.

Joe laughed lightly. "No man, I've never been here before" he replied.

Scott blushed. Gerry surreptitiously dug him in the side, just to let him know, in case he hadn't already realised, what a twat he was.

"I've been to Borneo" continued Joe, helpfully. "That's an island"

"Half an island" commented Clem.

"So why did you come here, Joe?" asked Toby, quickly covering Clem's pedantry.

"Why did I come here?" replied Joe. "Why has anyone come here? Dylan"

"I'm here for the Bonzo Dogs" quipped Gerry.

Joe nodded. "We'll take in the Bonzo Dogs too" he replied.

This response greatly pleased the four native boys. They were above flag-waving, but there was something personally reassuring in the acceptance of the quintessentially English Bonzos by a cool American.

"I'm looking forward to Tom Paxton" offered Toby.

Joe nodded. "Tom Paxton's cool" he replied.

This opened the gates to a farrago of favourites drawn from the weekend's line-up, all received with calm approval by Joe, who had seamlessly taken on the role of primary (or prep school) teacher.

"Ok, guys" he said eventually. "I have to love you and leave you" With practised ease he turned to Gerry and laid a hand on his shoulder. "Stay cool, man" he urged.

"I was only messing about!" laughed Gerry.

Joe nodded. "See you all around" he said, and the four boys all felt the same mild sinking feeling as he returned to his dugout.

"What a great guy" said Toby.

"Long way to come to see Dylan" pronounced Clem.

Toby shook his head. "Clem's just a Dylanphobe" he declared.

"Come on, Toby, that's not fair" responded Clem. "I'm prepared to give Dylan his due. I just don't subscribe to the hagiography that surrounds him"

"Hagiolatry" corrected Scott.

Up to this point Clem had barely noticed Scott. Now, however, their eyes met. Clem gave a little nod of approbation. They had bonded.

THREE

Maurice Moss's head appeared through the front flaps of the tent. "You're in luck" he said. "The sparks need another hand. Frankie White's gone down sick". Maurice mimed the sinking of a pint to clarify the nature of the illness.

Gerry checked his watch. Eight thirty in the morning. It had not been a good night – cold, restless, blighted by various strummers determined to give a foretaste of Dylan's impending gig.

"What - now?" asked Gerry.

"It's called the working day" replied Maurice.

Gerry nominated Scott, but Scott had a headache. He had tried to smoke a joint the night before, but unbeknown to him, had got ninety per cent Old Holborn and ten per cent card. He now assumed hash, rather than tobacco, made him nauseous.

"What have we got to do, anyway?" asked Gerry.

"Lump the gear, handle the sparks' tools, that kind of thing" replied Maurice.

"Handle the sparks' tools?" said Gerry. "Sounds like a job for Scott"

"I don't know anything about electricity" protested Scott, which of course was a lie, since he knew that electricity moved through the air in a thick blue arc when wires were unavailable.

"Listen, mate" replied Maurice. "No-one here knows about electricity"

Scott huddled beneath his makeshift sleeping-bag, wishing to hear no more of this. But Gerry was not about to let him off.

"Come on, Scott" he urged. "You owe me"

"What for?" complained Scott.

"All those drinks you've bummed!" replied Gerry.

"They're your dad's drinks!" protested Scott.

"You wouldn't have got them without me" replied Gerry.

"For fuck's sake!" said Maurice. "You wanted a job, I got you one! Now fucking get up, one of you, before I offer it to someone else!"

For a few moments, the wills of Scott and Gerry silently battled, then Scott roused himself. He knew that Gerry would rather destroy the whole expedition than give way to him.

Tom Croker was the man to whom Scott had to report. He was an unwilling spark, someone who had fallen into the job, a great Falstaffian heap of a man who would just as soon be expounding on Gibbons' Decline and Fall, preferably with someone who knew more about monkey shit than the Roman Empire. In the White brothers, his son Lewis and his sidekick Jim Dooley, he had just the right foils, good-humoured people who worked without complaint and would listen to his monologues without challenging his basic thesis that the human race, and particularly Tom Croker, was doomed.

Croker was not a bad boss, far happier at work than at rest, never short of a song, a joke or a packet of biscuits. He saved his malevolent side for his wife and family, was happy to delegate, and dished out praise generously. At the first sight of the callow newcomer he adopted a benign scepticism.

"Can you wire a plug?" he asked.

"I think so" replied Scott.

Croker checked Lewis's reactions. His son was hardly older than Scott, but his racing-driver eyes spoke of an infinitely more practical nature. Those eyes did not look impressed.

"Show him, Lew" said Croker.

Lewis took a Stanley knife, a pair of wire-trimmers and a piece of cable. In seconds he had stripped off the outer layer, cut the three wires to the appropriate lengths, fed the black into the neutral terminal, twisted the cable back to house the live and earth wires, then refitted the cable clip and reassembled the two halves of the plug. Scott at first tried to pay attention, but his mind soon strayed to the infamous Newport Folk Festival of 1965 when Dylan first went electric, and the competing accounts of just why and how badly he was booed. Scott's subsequent imitation of Lewis's plug-wiring was a horrible embarrassment and he was summarily despatched to be Matt White's ladder-carrier.

This wasn't such a terrible fate for Scott. Matt was easy company, a big man with a respectable mane of hair, wearing a half-tucked unironed shirt and trousers without flares. Unlike his brother Frank, he was a reliable worker, not so fond of the bottle. He and Frank had their own business, mainly house wiring, but Matt was happy to work for the bigger contractors when the jobs came along. Croker paid ok and took all the flak if anything went wrong, which suited Matt fine.

Given the complete lack of nous of his new assistant, it was fortunate that Matt was also a patient man, pleased to have some new company and a second pair of hands to help hump the coils of cable. They spent an easy enough time rigging catenaries across the toilet tents, then made their way towards Croker's backstage caravan for a cup of tea. As they reached the end of the arena, workers were busy erecting a white picket fence, enclosing a large semicircular area in front of the stage.

"What's that?" asked Scott.

"That's your VIP enclosure" explained Matt.

"Seriously?" said Scott.

"Word is there's a few nobs coming" replied Matt.

"What, and they're letting them have all the best seats?" said Scott.

"Them and the press" replied Matt.

"I can't believe that" said Scott.

Matt leaned towards him conspiratorially. "I wouldn't complain" said Matt. "You got a backstage pass"

"That'll get me in there, will it?" asked Scott.

Matt nodded.

"I don't want to go in there" said Scott.

Matt raised his eyebrows high, a look of supreme astonishment which put an end to the conversation. They repaired to the caravan where, without the spotlights and the cable clips between them, an embarrassed silence ensued.

"Did you know Bob Dylan was an electrician?" Scott eventually asked.

"Bob Dylan?" replied Matt. "Who's he?"

It was not a promising start to the conversation.

"You know" explained Scott. "Bob Dylan, who's headlining the festival"

Matt looked confused. "He's working with us?" he asked.

"No, no" replied Scott. "He *used* to work as an electrician. And his dad sold fridges"

Matt nodded. "Croker's got a fridge shop up on Swanmore Road" he remarked.

There was another silence.

"Have you really never heard of Bob Dylan?" asked Scott.

"What does he sing?" asked Matt.

"*Blowing in the Wind*" replied Scott.

"I've got you" replied Matt. "The protest singer"

"He's not just a protest singer" protested Scott.

Matt nodded. "Little yiddish feller" he said.

Scott's discomfort grew. "He is Jewish" he confirmed, ignoring the ugly epithet. "He doesn't practice though"

"Maybe that's why he sings so bad" replied Matt, taking a sip of tea.

Scott smiled, but only to be sociable. The situation was now sufficiently awkward for Scott to be planning exit routes, but it was about to get worse.

"Showbusiness is full of yids" commented Matt.

Scott wondered if he was being deliberately tested, in the way that racialists sometimes would – or did Matt live in a world where this kind of talk was considered perfectly normal? The Isle of Wight was a bit of a backwater, after all.

"I wouldn't call what Dylan does 'showbusiness'" Scott eventually replied.

"It's all showbusiness" said Matt.

"Not like Sunday Night at the London Palladium" replied Scott.

Matt gestured around at the half-built arena. "This is a show, isn't it?" he commented.

Scott viewed the lighting tower, the piles of PA speakers being assembled on the stage, and was lost for an answer.

"We always call it a show" continued Matt. "Ryde Town Hall…Island Industries Fair…"

"I've been to that" blurted Scott, thankful at last to find some common ground.

"Bob Dylan" muttered Matt, for no obvious reason, cutting off Scott's new line of approach and initiating another awkward silence.

"He's got a new album out" said Scott, eventually.

"Album?" queried Matt.

"LP" explained Scott.

"Oh, right" replied Matt. "Good, is it?"

"Not his best" said Scott.

"You don't think so?" asked Matt, without curiosity.

"It's country and western" replied Scott. "A bit of a departure for Dylan"

Matt nodded, took several sips of his tea, then casually lifted a pair of wire cutters. Between the blades was a neat round hole. "Look at that" he said. "Went through a live one yesterday"

Scott winced inwardly. Matt lowered the cutters and took several more sips of his tea. "I wouldn't say it was a departure" he commented.

"Sorry?" replied Scott.

"Everyone thinks Dylan got everything from Woody Guthrie" said Matt. "But there's a lot of Hank Williams in there too"

Scott made his way back towards the camp field at the end of the day with a workman's sense of satisfaction, but nagging worries as to why he had stereotyped Matt, and why Matt had stereotyped Dylan. Everyone knew that Dylan was Jewish of course, that his name was Zimmermann and his family had come from Russia or somewhere. It certainly cemented his appeal to Scott, who felt he also should have belonged to such a minority, not for reasons of liberal guilt or ideology, but simply because he was not like the majority, and could never rouse much enthusiasm for the casual racism which was *de rigeur* at Isaac Watts. The school, to its credit, had attempted to broaden their pupils' horizons by linking to a school in Nigeria, and for one term entertained a Nigerian teacher on exchange. Pupils had a good laugh at the school photo that year, the massed ranks of white faces interrupted by the sole exception of Mr Agube, the joke being that one face had failed to come out of the negative. Scott smiled along with the others, just as he smirked at the mention of jungle bunnies, the jokes about Derby Road, all the racist miscellanea cruising the veins of Southampton's finest school. But when Enoch Powell's speeches won him a fan club at the school, Scott felt nothing but contempt for the braying dupes who so easily bought the hate message. Couldn't they imagine this Enoch Powell as a master at the school, and where he would stand on the issues that affected them? Those mad-dog eyes promised nothing but misery, not only for the immigrants but for every youth who was hiding a wodge of hair behind his ears in the hope of future liberation.

The fact was, however, that Powell did have a following, and that following was growing, just as the counterculture was growing. Was Matt just winding him up, or was he part of that following? Was it possible that a man could know about Dylan's primary influences yet be anti-semitic?

Such thoughts propelled Scott back to the growing settlement of tents with renewed conviction. Forget the disgusting goulash and the funny ideas, these were people with good intentions. Scott wanted to be amongst them like being close to a fire, which appropriately was exactly what his new friends were building on his return.

Three unfamiliar figures had joined Gerry, Toby and Clem. A woman in her mid-twenties sat cross-legged on the ground, her skirt, singlet and cardigan all of a rainbow crochet, her arms dripping with bangles. She rocked to an inaudible tune, half-heartedly tossing a twig or two onto the fire. There was something of the silent movie star about her, Louise Brooks maybe, with the trace of a petulant frown. Alongside this woman, standing, were another woman and a man, again in their twenties, the man sporting a fair beard and heavy glasses, the woman rather taller, with a Lennon cap over unsmiling eyes. Both wore flared jeans and brown leather flying jackets with fake fur collars; both carried small rucksacks.

Scott was welcomed to the fold: over-firm handshakes from the greatcoat couple (Claus and Wendy), a greeting as weak as tissue from the rainbow woman (Cressida). Gaining in confidence, Scott flourished his backstage pass, which gained him gratifying kudos.

"I must have one of those" declared Cressida.

"I've only got this one" replied Scott.

"Please" insisted Cressida. "I'll give you anything"

Cressida's demand was as intense as her handshake was weak. Scott decided to change the subject, offering to cook some pasta and sauce, the prospect of which seemed miraculous to Toby. In truth, Scott barely had enough pasta for four people, but he was conscious of the unwritten rule of this new society, that if someone needed feeding, you fed them. As the others struggled to light the bonfire, Scott efficiently arranged his kitchen, an area in which he felt comfortable and purposeful. The water boiled, the fire took, and the growing group settled into an easy communion, watching the flames.

"So, you guys" began Claus, whose accent was German. "Are you looking forward to seeing Judas?"

"Oh, come on, Claus" said Wendy. "We've only just met these guys"

Claus turned to Wendy. "What do you think we should talk about?" he asked, irascibly.

"Stop being so heavy, Claus" replied Wendy.

There was an awkward silence.

"Who's Judas?" asked Toby.

"Dylan, of course" replied Claus.

"Why of course?" asked Gerry. A further day at the encampment had failed to soften his prickly defensiveness.

"Because he *is* a Judas" replied Claus.

"Why's that?" asked Toby, with a look of genuine concern.

"He betrayed the folk movement" replied Wendy, apparently forgetting her earlier strictures to Claus.

"Was he a member?" said Gerry.

"Don't try to make a joke of it" rasped Claus.

"Its up to him what he wants to play" asserted Gerry.

"He built his career on the folk movement" replied Claus. "He was nothing without the folk movement. He took our music, our values, our ideas. He grew fat on our money. Then he said fuck you"

"Maybe he just didn't want to get pigeonholed" suggested Toby.

"Except now he really is a pigeon in a hole" replied Wendy.

"Eh?" said Gerry.

"You don't understand this movement" asserted Claus.

"That's right, I don't" replied Gerry..

"Well don't be proud of it" said Claus.

"I agree with Gerry" added Toby. "Saying you can't use an electric guitar is ridiculous. You can't live in the past"

"Yeah, like the people who said rock and roll was jungle music" added Gerry.

"We don't say that" replied Claus. "We are against commercial music which is just filling the minds of the youth with pap. We are for music that makes you think".

There was a short pause, then Cressida piped up: "I blame Shirley" she declared.

Gerry laughed. "Who the fuck's Shirley?" he asked.

"The so-called Sara Dylan" replied Cressida. "That's her real name, you know. Shirley. She's a fake. It was after he met her he sold out"

"Yes, there could be something in that" responded Wendy. "What can we expect when his muse is a Playboy bunny?".

"I know for a fact that's what happened" asserted Cressida.

"For a fact?" replied Gerry. "What do you mean, for a fact?"

"He told me" said Cressida.

"What, in bed, was it?" scoffed Gerry.

"The back of a van, actually" replied Cressida, meeting his eyes.

"Bit of a cliché" mused Toby.

"It's what musicians travel in" replied Cressida, scornfully.

"I thought he had his own plane" said Scott.

"Not when I knew him" replied Cressida.

"You never knew him!" scoffed Gerry.

Cressida turned on him. "I could tell you some intimate details about Dylan that prove I've been with him" she snapped.

"Such as?" said Gerry.

"A birthmark on his arse for a start" asserted Cressida.

"Yeah, well how we going to dispute that?" replied Gerry. "We're not going to see his arse"

The conversation seemed to have arrived at a natural hiatus, but Claus was determined to restart the debate. "Ewan MacColl called Dylan "tenth rate drivel"" he asserted.

"Who's Ewan MacColl?" asked Gerry.

"Who is Ewan MacColl?" scoffed Claus. "Ewan MacColl is probably the greatest songwriter in the world"

"I've never heard of him" replied Gerry.

"So?" said Claus.

"What's he written?" asked Gerry.

"Well, there is *Dirty Old Town*, for a start" said Claus.

Gerry snorted with laughter. "You think *Dirty Old Town* is better than Dylan?" he scoffed.

"For sure" asserted Claus.

Gerry shook his head in disbelief. "What are you here for, if you hate Dylan so much?" he asked.

Claus opened his rucksack and pulled out a sheaf of *Morning Star*s. "Want to buy one?" he asked.

"Not if you write the music reviews" replied Gerry.

Suddenly Clem began to recite:

"Joe Stalin was a mighty man and a mighty man was he

He led the Soviet people on the road to victory"

"What's that?" asked Cressida.

"Oh, he's just taking the piss" scoffed Claus.

"Your hero wrote it" replied Clem.

"He's not my hero" snapped Claus.

"They don't understand, Claus" said Wendy, laying a calming hand on Claus's forearm.

"And talking of people changing their names" continued Clem, "wasn't Ewan MacColl christened Jimmie Miller?"

"Oh, and so what?" replied Claus.

At this point Scott could hold his silence no more. It had bothered him greatly that he had not challenged Matt earlier in the day. Now that his confidence had grown, he saw his opportunity to step in, to show an example, to be like Joe.

"Come on, man" he said. "Food's ready, let's eat it in peace"

There was a short silence, then a splutter of laughter from Gerry.

"What?" challenged Scott.

"You said 'man'" scoffed Gerry.

"Did I?" said Scott, reddening.

"You've never said 'man' in your life" replied Gerry.

"Got the plates, Toby?" asked Scott. He hated Gerry, hated him with a passion, wished for all the world he'd come without him and resolved to dump him at the first opportunity. With Gerry around, there was no room for growth, no chance of becoming that greater person.

"Yeah, let's eat" said Toby. He handed round out a range of improvised eating vessels, from tin plates to wooden salad bowls. Scott doled out the paltry meal, which was met with ridiculous overenthusiasm by all but Gerry.

"Sorry man, what was your name?" asked Claus.

"Scott" replied Scott.

"Thanks, Scott" said Claus, emphatically and with genuine warmth. He took a few mouthfuls then swallowed hard and laid down his fork. "So now we have *Nashville Skyline*" he pronounced. "Fucking country and western"

"Claus" said Wendy. "Shut up"

Claus had not always been so cantankerous. His spleen was born of the frustration that rebellion was in the air everywhere, yet the party was leaking members like a sieve. Since the Soviet tanks had rolled into Prague, Claus and his comrades had been fighting a losing battle while every band of confused libertarians or renegade Trotskyists were recruiting hand over fist. Claus's uncle Uwe, a Volkswagen car worker and IG Metall shop steward, had encouraged Claus to study in Britain where the CPGB, unlike the German KPD, was legal. In the wake of May 1968 in France, Uwe was convinced that capitalism was finished, but Claus's doubts were growing. It wasn't just the Trotskyists who were critical of the Soviet Union, but also a sizeable faction within the CPGB itself.

Now the rift ran right through Claus's own relationship. At first, both he and Wendy shared the view that the rebelling East Europeans, with their free healthcare, universal employment and dirt-cheap housing, were merely the victims of CIA propaganda and dirty tricks. Back in January, however, when Jan Palach set himself on fire in Wenceslas Square, that line no longer squared with Wendy's intuition. Contented people did not turn themselves into human torches.

As yet, however, there had been no split in the CPGB, nor between Claus and Wendy. But the tensions, between two such intense people, were growing. They had come to the island ostensibly to recruit, with an unspoken understanding this would help recement their relationship. Failure, however, was likely to have the opposite effect, especially with everyone else seemingly intent on having the time of their lives.

Claus and Wendy, therefore, were running a slide-ruler over every new acquaintance, noting their opinions, their receptiveness, their fortitude. Around that night's camp fire prospects were not great. Gerry was self-orientated, a blasé motormouth full of reactionary ideas. Cressida was a Dylan obsessive with a screw loose, entirely apolitical except for the usual tiresome feminist trappings. Toby was better, an idealist at least, but utopian and anarchistic, unsurprising given his bourgeois background. Clem - there was someone with some familiarity with Marxism, except he already knew too much and was almost certainly infected with Trotskyism, an irreversible condition in Claus's experience.

No, Scott was the only interesting one. A moral fire was smouldering there, but his direction was uncertain and his ideas heterogenous. He looked a little effeminate and had briefly touched on the Stonewall riots during the evening's conversation, but that did not necessarily mean he was only concerned with petit-bourgeois struggles such as the battle for gay rights. Scott was worth spending a little time with, first of all to ascertain his opinions on the Morning Star which he had so generously been given free of charge.

FOUR

Scott was flattered by the warmth and generosity of Claus the next morning, less so by the attentions of Gerry, who, uninvited, insisted on accompanying him to work with Matt. Gerry's motivation was a backstage pass, and despite there being no need for an extra hand, he did not fail in his endeavour. Gerry had learnt a lot from his old man: how to turn on the charm for those who paid the rent, no matter how worthless they might be. Every barfly at the Royal George was convinced Bill Roche was his best friend, little suspecting the withering scorn they suffered the moment the pub doors were locked. Whether Matt could judge the falsity of Gerry's bonhomie it was hard to say, but once the golden ticket was in Gerry's hand, this was of little concern to him.

Matters were hotting up fast. As Scott and Gerry left the arena that afternoon, the hundreds had become thousands, the thousands tens of thousands. Word was there would be a free concert that evening, the Nice topping the bill, and the sense of expectation was tangible. Biblical droves drifted up Palmers Road like refugees from the uptight world. Bodies thronged the information stall and the disco tent, meeting, greeting, laying claim to sleeping spaces. Alternative customers swarmed around the row of temporary shops. The happening was happening, a new city the like of which had never been seen in Europe, let alone the Isle of Wight.

Scott, however, was not ready for these numbers. He'd carved himself a niche amongst the early arrivals and felt comfortable there. Suddenly he felt lost again, overwhelmed, convinced everyone knew what they were doing there except him. He soon lost Gerry in the crowd, and rather than make his way back to a now teeming camp field, began to wander aimlessly.

There was one spot which had drawn Scott for the past two days, and it was to the makeshift record store that he now repaired. Once again, under the pungent scent of joss sticks, his eyes fell on one particular album, the controversial *Blind Faith,* with its (allegedly) thirteen-year-old cover girl, toplessly clasping a phallic silver spaceplane. It seemed all wrong to draw attention to such groundbreaking music in such a crass manner, a manner designed to attract the most backward elements of society, men who would just stare blatantly at the half-formed teenager, rather than opening the gatefold repeatedly, as Scott did, to pretend to be interested in the track listing.

It was as he glazedly studied the design of Blind Faith's space vessel that Scott became aware of a second pair of eyes perusing the album, slightly to the right of his own and not that far behind. He turned his head to see a shambolic figure in a greatcoat, tall but hunched, chaotic sheepdog hair almost hiding a faint benign smile.

"Ginger Baker" mumbled the figure, in a cracked northern accent.

Scott nodded, surreptitiously opening the gatefold to study the track listing he had long ago committed to memory.

"Ginger Baker and Eric Clapton" continued the figure. "Wow. No wonder they call it a supergroup"

"But they were together in Cream" replied Scott.

Greatcoatman's smile faded as his mind struggled to come to terms with this startling revelation. A lightbulb appeared and the smile returned, broader than before, a smile of childish delight.

"You're fucking right!" he laughed.

Scott turned back to the album, hoping the conversation was at an end, but greatcoatman remained, just a little too advanced into Scott's personal space, little grunts of laughter continuing like aftershocks.

Suddenly there was a cry. "Dave! What the fuck are you doing here?"

A young woman stood behind them. She wore a grandad vest and jeans, with short dark hair cut Julie Driscoll style over what might have been a pretty, catlike face were it not for the thunderous frown upon it.

"Oh, hi Jayne" said greatcoatman.

"I told you to wait by the disco tent!" snapped Jayne.

"Sorry" said Dave.

"Those toilets are a fucking disgrace" said Jayne.

"Fucking...armageddon" said Dave.

In a flash Jayne's demeanour changed. A huge spontaneous grin lit up her face. "Armageddon!" she laughed.

The unexpected combination of surliness and humour in the young woman instantly attracted Scott. She really was quite nice looking, with a long pale neck, though this was angled forward from her back, lending her an ungainly posture.

"He's not bothering you, is he?" she suddenly asked.

Scott flushed. His fumbling fingers buried *Blind Faith* behind *Wasa Wasa* by the Edgar Broughton Band. "No, he's alright" he blurted.

"He's been stoned since the moon landing" explained Jayne, with another grin.

"Did my head in" concurred Dave.

"He wants to go up there" said Jayne.

"I am going up there" asserted Dave.

"It's not going to happen, Dave" replied Jayne.

"It could happen" said Dave, "if the Yanks and the Ruskies worked together"

"Dave," replied Jayne, "the only reason the Yanks went to the moon was to prove they were better than the Ruskies"

"So?" said Dave. "They've proved it now"

Jayne turned to Scott. "Dave doesn't understand the Cold War" she commented.

"I just want peace" said Dave.

"You smoke too much dope" replied Jayne.

"If everyone smoked dope" replied Dave, "there would be peace"

Jayne sighed wearily. "Yeah, yeah" she scoffed. "Try telling my brother"

"Your brother's a psycho" replied Dave.

"Yeah" agreed Jayne. "A psycho with a gun"

Dave nodded emphatically. Scott's adrenaline flow, which had just about sputtered out after the rearrangement of the LPs, resumed its regular course. The grotesque murder of Sharon Tate in Death Valley had been in his mind frequently over the past weeks. He imagined the terror that was still gripping Hollywood and suddenly wondered just how safe they were in these open fields, a vulnerable mass vilified by the haters and baiters of the mainstream world.

"So who's this brother?" Scott asked.

"Don't worry" replied Jayne, reading his mind. "They've packed him off to Northern Ireland"

To Scott's dismay, that was evidently the end of their conversation. Jayne fell into a private conflab with Dave then without farewell began moving off in the direction of the nearest gate to the arena, where a large queue had formed.

As Jayne and Dave walked away, Scott experienced a kind of epiphany. It was impossible that nature was already adapting people for sitting on a hard field all day, yet Jayne was most wondrously equipped for such a purpose, to such an extent that Scott was filled with a terrible yearning, in which desires for sex and comfort intertwined, and though he'd only just met Jayne, the suitability of her bosom for a pillow was unquestionable. He followed the pair, impatiently burrowing among the multitude, frantically seeking a gambit with which to reopen the conversation. Was it cool to chat someone up at a festival? Shouldn't they just relate, get rapping, make a connection? But how did you do that if you weren't all sitting round a bonfire smoking hash?

Scott had neither the time nor the know-how to come to a suitable conclusion. Reaching the pair, he tapped Jayne on the shoulder and as she turned, somewhat surprised, blurted "Do you think it's a good thing, sending the troops to Ireland?"

"Pardon?" replied Jayne.

Scott had struck the wrong note and knew it, but there was no turning back. "My grandad was in the army in Ireland" he continued, "but both his brothers died in the trenches and he got off on compassionate grounds".

Jayne began to look uneasy. "Are you getting in the queue for the Nice?" she asked.

"Yeah, do you think they'll do *America*?" replied Scott.

"Probably" said Jayne, looking away. The three of them were now enveloped by the growing queue, an island of tension in the hopeful horde.

"They never found one of the brothers" continued Scott.

Jayne folded her arms, clearly wishing him gone, while Dave reprised the famous melody from *West Side Story* as adapted by Keith Emerson. The situation seemed hopeless, but fate was about to deal Scott a generous hand. Approaching from the camp field was none other than Clem, alone, a little disorientated, and glad to catch sight of Scott. Scott for his part was as eager as a dog at the sight of his master, shocking Clem by the sudden intimacy he assumed as he clapped him on the back with salutary greetings.

"Clem!" he declared. "Where's Toby?"

"Dunno, I've lost him" replied Clem, unsure whether to extricate himself from the unexpected embrace.

"Jayne, this is Clem" announced Scott, arm still locked round Clem's shoulder.

"Pleased to meet you" mumbled Jayne.

"Where's Claus and Wendy?" asked Scott. "I promised Claus I'd have a drink with him this evening. Is Cressida still about? I hope Joe knows the Bonzos are on"

Clem eased himself away. "Dunno" he said. "Where's Gerry?"

"Search me" replied Scott. "We're not Siamese twins"

Scott glanced back at Jayne, checking she had cottoned on to the size of his social circle. "This is Dave" she said, flatly.

"Oh yeah, sorry, this is Dave, Clem" blabbed Scott.

Dave shook Clem's hand. "Good to meet you, man" he mumbled.

"Why don't you come in with us, Clem?" asked Scott.

Jayne could hardly have failed to notice Scott's presumptious little pronoun, but other than a quick glance at Dave, she did not react. The presence of Clem did at least give her some insulation from Scott, and once the music had started, his random babble would hopefully stop. Jayne had spent enough time around the fringes of society to meet plenty of trying people; like dogs, they simply had to be well handled.

The crowd was growing impatient. Since today's festival was free, there was no need for any delay in processing the customers. The workers around the ticket booths were simply waiting for the go-ahead, and when it finally came, the dam broke with ecstatic fervour. With the Great Awakening's *Amazing Grace* booming from the monster PA, the crowd burst from the three gates and streamed across the empty field in a surge of unstoppable energy. The great festival had begun with a footrace.

Scott's competitive instincts were immediately engaged. He had managed 69.5 for the 440 yards at the last sports day, a key performance in securing Clausentum the House Shield. Inspired by the choral guitars of *Amazing Grace* he sped mercilessly past a hundred hapless hippies, only to realise that he had become dangerously isolated from Jayne. Turning back he was infuriated to realise that their progress was impeded by the most ridiculously languid lope from Clem, whose bendy pipe-cleaner legs and backward-leaning demeanour resembled something from a Robert Crum cartoon. Unmoved by Scott's yells of exhortation, Clem maintained the same steady pace, while every spaz and fatso in Woodside Bay passed them en route to a better view.

It was all too bad, but it was about to get even worse as Dave suddenly lurched to the ground. Jayne rushed to his side and when Scott arrived was showing grave concern.

"Dave!" she implored. "Dave, are you alright?"

Dave lay face down and motionless. Suddenly, however, he rolled over onto his back and began to giggle uncontrollably.

"Fuck me, Dave, I thought you'd hurt yourself!" said Jayne.

Dave's knees rose towards his chin as the spasms of laughter overwhelmed him. Scott felt a surge of hatred for him, partly because he'd lost them the best views of the stage, partly because it was possible, however inexplicable, that he was Jayne's boyfriend.

FIVE

The Bonzos did not disappoint. Where Woodstock was fired up by Country Joe flaying the Vietnam war, the Isle of Wight was charged by blue men singing the whites and Roger Ruskin Spear playing the trouser press. Bonhomie spread across the field, darkness fell and the great floodlights swung into action as the Nice took the stage. Keith Emerson attacked his organ and the night went magic, even at 2 and 6 for a yogurt.

No-one felt this magic more than Scott. To his right was Clem, rolling expert eight-rizla joints, and to his left Jayne, toking on these with a religious intensity. There was something so sexual in the way she closed her eyes and held the smoke in her lungs, all the more so because Jayne did not do eye flashes, coy looks, or any of the other conventional flirty routines. Jayne was straight as a die, except, as Scott discovered that evening, she lived in a squat near Regents Park with an ever-changing cast of freaks and dropouts with whom she apparently coexisted quite happily.

But what exactly was the nature of her coexistence with Dave? As the night wore on, there was no snuggling up together, no whispered conversations, nothing that could identify them clearly as lovers. But when Dave struggled to get out of a jersey, Jayne helped him in a matter-of-fact way that suggested such contact was not abnormal. And when Jayne disappeared to buy her fatally expensive yogurt, Dave looked round time and again to check her progress. If they were friends, they were friends of a type Scott had never met before, not that that was saying much after five years at Isaac Watts.

At least Jayne was talking to Scott now, voluntarily, and not in response to observations about the First World War. Music and hash oiled the conversation, they laughed in the same places at the Bonzos, and Scott began to sense that a chemistry really did exist between them. Somehow he had to ensure they would meet up again, no certainty in a crowd which could have filled the Dell four times over. Dave and Jayne were duly invited to a communal campsite breakfast, and just to make sure they would find the right place, Scott and Clem would visit their sleeping berths next morning, half way down on the left hand side of the disco tent as long as no dancing freaks had kicked away their sleeping bags.

The new world, however, was not a great respecter of plans, and sure enough, next morning, a bomb blast could not have woken Clem. Scott headed alone to the disco tent, found no sign of Dave and Jayne, but did come across a machine pumping out gallons of foam into a nearby field. Semi-naked revellers were baptising themselves in the froth, and lo and behold, there was Dave, stripped to his undies, slapping suds into his face.

Heart pumping, Scott sought out Jayne, half hoping, half fearing she was part of this ritual. And if she was, what should he do? The more abandonment he saw, the more he felt his bowels contract and his chest tighten. Scott's head was back on the mainland, five years back, a shivering firstie baulking at pulling down his shorts and running into the shower after the other boys. To

Scott, running that shower was like running the bulls in Pamplona, especially when the hand of Arnie Pugh rested on the temperature control, a hand which was famed for its mercurial twists from hot to cold and back again.

Nor was it comforting to feel the eyes of Arnie Pugh on your half-formed body, for those eyes seldom strayed from the line of naked boys escaping back into the changing room, glistening with water, teeth chattering, parts jangling. The grammar school ethos encouraged those teachers who loved a little power, to witness the boys all rise as the master entered the room, to feel the boys' fear at the thought of detention, to know no boy would openly accuse one of what everybody knew to be true. After all, it was traditional discipline which encouraged parents to desire an Isaac Watts education for their beloved boy children, and Arnie Pugh was a wholehearted dispenser of that.

Dr Snode had a different style. Lying in wait like a predatory spider outside the Maths Room, he would seize and quickly enfold his victim in his powerful arms, holding them in this fatal embrace for ten, maybe fifteen minutes while conducting a one-sided conversation in his rich and insistent baritone before releasing the mortally embarrassed morsel to enjoy the ridicule of his peers for the remainder of his school life.

Scott had fallen victim to Snode more than once. For all Gerry's taunts about his supposedly odd appearance, Scott, especially when pubescent, was actually quite a pretty boy, with intelligent blue eyes and pouting red lips, not unlike Snode's own sons and very much to their father's taste. Snode called Scott his special friend, bringing his waxy, strangely unlined face horribly close to Scott's ear as he asked after his family or queried his opinions on the 1967 Summer of Love.

Snode's proclivities, needless to say, had not gone unnoticed in the Isaac Watts staffroom, but the idea of disciplining such an eminent mathematician, one of the jewels in the school's crown, was unthinkable. Snode was eventually promoted to Head of Sixth Form, but this manoeuvre failed to stop his hulking embrace of the younger boys or the memories of helplessness of those grown older.

Now Scott had to put his own memories of Pugh and Snode behind him. There was nothing shameful in the body; what was happening before him was liberation. True, it was also young adults behaving like children, but that was what the uptight world most feared: joy, spontanaeity… vulnerability.

Scott's fingers toyed with a shirt button. The weather was rather cold. No, he couldn't do it. And then he saw Jayne.

To Scott's relief, Jayne also stood on the sidelines, arms folded, watching Dave's antics from a safe distance while shouting out a few words of encouragement. For a brief second her eyes flashed in Scott's direction, revealing that she knew he was there, but she made no acknowledgement. Undeterred, Scott leaned forward and practised a large, slow wave of the hand within her peripheral vision. Getting no response, he moved a few yards closer and did it again, then again, at a distance she couldn't possibly ignore.

"Oh, hello" she said.

"Not going in?" he asked, cheerfully.

"They want to watch they don't catch cold" she remarked.

Scott secretly delighted in this response. Jayne seemed so sure about things, her flat factual manner lending her words a weight no BBC newsreader could hope for. If Jayne was ok about staying out of the foam, it must have been alright for Scott to stay out of the foam. They continued to watch the cavorting, happy for the happy people, but Scott wished more than anything to be alone with Jayne, away from these hundred thousand revellers, maybe down on the hard at Hamble with a bottle of Carafino.

It was a fair bet that the couple on the far side of the foam had no such wish. They were wrapped around each other's slithery bodies, snogging in a manner that suggested they didn't intend to stop there.

"They're having fun" remarked Jayne.

"Sure you don't fancy it?" asked Scott.

Jayne turned, astonished. "What?" she said.

"Going in the foam, I mean" blurted Scott, blushing hard.

"Oh" replied Jayne. "I wondered what you were saying for a second"

Scott's embarrassment was thankfully short-lived as Dave's shouts for attention were decoded by Jayne. "Oh shit" she said. "Dave's lost his glasses"

Dave's arms flailed hopelessly in the foam. He was clearly helpless without his specs.

"Here goes nothing" said Jayne. She kicked off her sandals and wriggled out of her jeans, revealing two pale and sturdy legs, not perhaps to every man (or woman)'s taste, but most decidedly to Scott's. As she launched herself into the foam, his inhibitions were suddenly overtaken by an unassailable desire to curry favour with her; within seconds he had followed suit, barely aware that he had rashly chosen his most tasteless underpants that day, a pair of orange C&A specials with white y-front piping.

The proverbial needle in the haystack was not that much harder a target than Dave's specs in a sea of foam, especially with revellers plunging about on all sides. However, they identified the general area in which the glasses had been lost, divided it up into segments, and swept the area as thoroughly as possible. Determined to prove his worth, Scott pressed his head right down into the froth, submarine style, finally emerging to see Jayne just a few feet away, her attention distracted from the spec hunt by the former snogging couple who were now completely naked and shagging furiously.

Scott had once found himself alone in a room with a breastfeeding woman and was now faced with the same dilemma, whether to look slightly to one side and pretend everything was normal when it clearly wasn't, or whether to stare directly at the blatant sight in order to prove it was ok with him.

In the end fate made the choice for him. Seeking purchase in the slippery suds as her manfriend thundered into her, the transported woman seized hold of Scott's ankle, burying her nails into his flesh with unconscious ferocity. Scott could not stifle the yell of pain this necessitated, his subsequent pleas to be released merging with the general cacophony of the lovemaking and casual applause from onlookers.

Eventually Scott was mercifully released, only at this point realising just how much he had contributed to Jayne's morning. Tears brimmed from her eyes as, bent double with hilarity, she welcomed Scott back to dry land, informing him for his added pleasure that Dave had realised he had not been wearing his glasses all along, and that these were safely stowed in his greatcoat pocket.

"I could have blood poisoning" complained Scott, examining his wounds and redoubling Jayne with laughter. Seeing his petulant frown, however, she wiped her eyes and laid a consoling hand on his shoulder. "Thanks anyway" she said.

"It's the foam that stings" commented Scott.

Jayne stood back a little and perused Scott's injuries. "You should get some new underpants" she remarked.

"They're not mine" blurted Scott, unthinkingly.

"In that case" replied Jayne, "You should get some new friends"

"I didn't get them from a friend" said Scott.

"Don't tell me you found them in a bin" said Jayne.

"They're Dylan's" replied Scott.

"Oh aye?" said Jayne.

"According to Cressida" added Scott.

"Who's Cressida?" asked Jayne.

"This woman that's been hanging round with us" said Scott. "She reckons she's had a relationship with Dylan. She kept his undies for a memento"

Jayne was not the kind of person to afford such an idea credulity, but nevertheless, for the sake of sport, chose to suspend disbelief. "Do they have special properties?" she asked.

"Possibly" replied Scott. "I wrote a good protest song this morning".

"Must be an old pair" remarked Jayne.

Scott considered putting his trousers on again, but had actually started to quite enjoy his newfound sense of freedom. His bare legs were for once making him feel like the vanguard of this new movement. "Are you still coming for breakfast?" he asked.

"Ok" replied Jayne.

Scott hummed with excitement. "I'll do you a full English" he promised.

"How patriotic" replied Jayne.

"Seriously, I'll do you bacon, eggs, tomatoes and mushrooms" enthused Scott.

Jayne's smile faded. "If you feed me dead pig" she remarked, "I shall stuff it straight up your arse"

Scott, whose ankle was still very sore, took stock of the new threat. "Reading between the lines" he responded, "are you a vegetarian?"

"You're very perceptive" replied Jayne.

"It's the underpants" quipped Scott.

Jayne folded her arms and gave Scott a clinical once-over. "Your legs are better than Dylan's" she remarked.

"How do you know?" asked Scott.

"Aha" said Jayne, tapping her nose.

"Don't tell Cressida" said Scott.

"I must meet this Cressida" replied Jayne.

At this point Scott chanced a glance at Dave. He was standing not far from Jayne, drying his hair with a t-shirt, and could hardly have failed to notice Jayne's compliment on his legs, nor the spark that had ignited between them. But Dave smiled benignly, which either meant he did not care that Jayne was being pursued, or knew that Scott was no serious threat to their powerful and inscrutable bond.

Back at base camp rumours were rife. Matt White was proving to be a mine of information to Gerry, faithfully relaying everything he'd heard from the festival organisers and their minions. Some of these revelations were trivial, like the fact there was a tent backstage entirely filled with Danone yogurt. Sometimes, however, they were worthy contenders for the newspaper front pages – all those papers were well represented on site, desperate for stories that would appal and simultaneously excite their equally hypocritical readers.

Such a rumour had reached Gerry's ears that morning. "The Who aren't coming" was how he greeted Scott.

"Why not?" asked Scott.

"They found out how much Dylan's getting" continued Gerry. "Now they want more"

"How much is Dylan getting?" asked Scott.

"Thirty five thou" replied Gerry.

"Thirty five thou?" repeated Scott, aghast.

"Won't be protesting about that, will he?" quipped Gerry.

Scott took the news like a blow. Dylan taking thirty-five thousand? It was a sum as distant as the moon. "How much are the Who getting?" he asked.

"About five hundred, apparently" replied Gerry. He explained that the Who had signed the contract before Woodstock, which the sucker organisers had declared a free festival just as they were forking out $11 grand for them. Woodstock was a triumph for the Who and they now expected the same treatment everywhere.

Scott wasn't entirely surprised. Despite the band's festival appearances, it wasn't hard to imagine those Fawley skinheads with a Who album nestling alongside their Trojan ska. Not that that would bother Gerry, for whom the Who could do no wrong. Like Townshend, Gerry had a fast right hand and could play the guitar intro to *Pinball Wizard* like a demon. It was, indeed, his favourite party piece, winning the admiration of males and females alike, though their appreciation tended to pall as Gerry introduced his follow-up, recreating Entwistle's Wagnerian bass via his anal sphincter. Entwistle was Gerry's particular hero: like Andy Fraser, he was an effortlessly skilful bassist, but one whose charisma was all the greater for standing menacingly still with an air of a knuckledustered doorman.

Discussion of the Who's possible non-appearance was the main topic of conversation as the various campers gathered for breakfast. Scott's misgivings were shared by Toby. "I don't think it'll be any great loss if they don't play" he asserted.

"Why not?" said Gerry.

"They're not what the festival's about" replied Toby.

"Who says?" asked Gerry.

"They're not part of the underground" replied Toby.

Gerry pulled a pained face. "It's called the Isle of Wight Festival of Music" he pointed out. "Not the Isle of Wight Festival of the Underground"

"They did write a rock opera" commented Clem.

"Yeah" said Toby. "Because they were going out of fashion and thought they could cash in on the new movement"

"Have you actually heard *Tommy*?" challenged Gerry.

"I've heard some of it, yeah" replied Toby, defensively.

"It's fucking good music" said Gerry.

"I'm not saying it hasn't -" began Toby.

"There's stuff in *Tommy* that no-one has ever written about before" continued Gerry.

"That doesn't - " began Toby.

"*Acid Queen*, you can't say that's mainstream"

"Mmm..." said Toby, grimacing, as if to say Gerry wasn't quite getting the point.

"You think no-one's alternative unless they wear scheisting flowers in their hair" remarked Gerry.

"There's more to being alternative than being stoned" countered Toby.

"That's what I'm saying!" responded Gerry.

"You just said *Acid Queen* wasn't mainstream" replied Toby.

"Let's talk about something else" said Cressida, who had just dragged herself out of her tent and had a headache.

Claus and Wendy joined the fold, and a difficult silence ensued. Claus and Wendy weren't really fitting in, yet were doggedly determined to be part of the group. Claus, who hadn't caught much of the conversation, expressed enthusiasm for the first line of *Substitute*, the one about the plastic spoon, and this non-sequitur seemed to quell the debate entirely. Scott's hankering for Jayne returned, along with some concern with what he could feed her. But as soon as he broached the subject of breakfast there were stirrings at the other end of his canal, the first stirrings since they'd arrived on site and ones he had very much feared due to the armageddon previously mentioned in the communal toilets.

There was no ignoring this call. Secreting a few tissues in his pocket, Scott made his way towards one of the toilet tents, fearing the worst.

Scott was not disappointed. He hadn't expected the toilets to be four star, but he did imagine they might be like the toilets on trains, with a dingy situpon and an open drop to who-knows-where, maybe a cesspit someone had dug. His heart sank when, behind a flimsy cubicle, he found nothing but a chemical toilet, in which were the final products of at least fifty festival-goers. The stench of shit and formaldehyde was itself enough to make a sensitive soul wretch, but the thought of hovering over a communal stool pool was Scott's ultimate nightmare.

Scott prepared the throne with a few sheets of Izal and tried to reason with himself. Shitting was a basic bodily function: hadn't he just overcome one inhibition in the foam, and was it so hard to shed another? Didn't the Romans sit in circles amiably chatting as they dumped? Then again, most of them lived before two thousand years of Christianity, war between the spirit and the flesh, God and the turd.

Yes, that was it, the Christians were to blame! All those morbid hymns they'd made Scott sing, all those futile prayers, and now they were stopping him from having a shit!

There was only one answer. Scott had to distance himself from the situation, stop thinking about the leavings below him and the guys next door. Think of the Saints. What a season it had been…seventh in the first division…highest in the club's history…Ted Bates, WHAT a servant…Terry Paine UP the right wing, should still be playing for England…John McGrath, NO-ONE got past him and lived…Mick Channon, WHAT a prospect, who said Chivers couldn't be replaced?…Ron Davies, BEST centre forward in Europe…FOUR goals against Man U, all made by Sydenham…JOHN Sydenham, fastest wing in history…those AMAZING runs…GO ON, John! GO ON! Up the touchline! Ball's COMING …Ball's COMING…RON'S HEAD WILL DO THE REST!

Damn. Dispossessed.

Scott hurried back across the camping field in increasing desperation. The motion he had proposed could not be removed from the agenda, and it was a matter of the utmost urgency that he retrieve more bogroll from his tent and find some cover of nature in order to ensure its passage. Approaching base camp, he was grateful to see that all but Toby and Clem had disappeared, but not so pleased them locked in yet another debate which he would surely not escape.

Sure enough, Toby beckoned urgently at their new friend as he stumbled in an oddly twisted configuration towards them. "Scott!" he called. "Come and settle an argument"

"I'm in a hurry" replied Scott, hobbling quickly towards his tent.

"Scott" pronounced Toby, laying a hand on Scott's shoulder. "Everything's cool. How can you be in a hurry?"

A simple statement of fact would have explained exactly why speed was of the essence, but Scott's toiletry inhibitions extended beyond the act itself to mere discussion. He therefore stood helplessly, a victim of Toby's intimacy and purpose.

"Clem maintains the completely untenable position that *John Wesley Harding* is Dylan's greatest album" announced Toby.

"It is" confirmed Clem.

"If you took a straw poll at this festival, ninety per cent would say *Bringing It All Back Home*" declared Toby.

"Oh, come on, Toby" scoffed Clem. "You can't say that"

"I'd put money on it" replied Toby.

"Toby" continued Clem, "you do not have access to the minds of a hundred thousand people"

"What do you think, Scott?" asked Toby.

Toby's desperate situation was becoming more critical by the second. Cogent thought was virtually impossible.

"Dunno, tell you later" he blurted.

"No, Scott" pressed Toby, replacing his hand on Scott's shoulder with greater insistence. "You can't sit on the fence"

For a brief second this image became very real to Scott, conflated with the act he needed so badly to perform.

"Can you name one decent track on *John Wesley Harding*?" Toby insisted.

"Not right now" blurted Scott.

"Oh, come on, Scott" replied Clem. "What about *All Along the Watchtower*?"

Both Alleynians focussed intently on Scott's response. Had he actually heard the original of *All Along the Watchtower*, or was he seduced, like most people, by Hendrix's far superior version? And why did the question produce such suffusion in his face, a look of pain almost, as if the quandary over *John Wesley Harding* was almost the quandary of life itself?

Down in Scott's lower bowel, matters were resolving themselves as speed. The prospect of securing the bogroll and making it to a suitable copse was now zero, leaving Scott with only one option: to evacuate in his tent.

"Just a second" he blabbed, fumblingly opening the front flaps and scrambling inside.

"No good hiding in there" teased Toby.

Scott was oblivious, his only thought to find a suitable receptacle for the deed. There in the corner of the desperately cramped accommodation lay Scott and Gerry's sole cooking vessel, a battered aluminium milk saucepan in which the pair prepared their nightly posset. Lacking an alternative, Scott put aside fears of sacrilege, pulled down his jeans and pants and squatted over the said pan. It was an instable arrangement, with Scott's head pressed sideways against the ridge of the tent and his right hand gaining poor purchase on a half-emptied rucksack. His body had made up his own mind, however, and the waste began to issue without delay.

Halfway through this process of elimination, however, Scott was appalled to hear a third voice outside the tent. Jayne's voice.

"Is Scott around?" it enquired.

Scott's bowels seized.

"He's in his tent" replied Toby.

It was a hopeless situation. The turd had gone too far to be withdrawn, but not far enough to drop. Never had purgatory been better defined.

"Scott?" called Jayne. "Where's this breakfast?"

"Just lying down!" blurted Scott.

"Get yourself out here, we're starving!" said Jayne.

"No!" cried Scott.

"I'll come in then" replied Jayne.

"*No!*" bawled Scott.

There was a moment's silence, but thank God, no head appeared through the flaps. Jayne had been drinking, a small flask of poteen brought to the squat by some Irish friends, and was at that moment averse to sudden movements or bending down.

"I do eat eggs" said Jayne.

"Uh-huh" grunted Scott.

"Dave'll eat anything" added Jayne.

There was a low murmur, at which point Scott realised Dave was also outside the tent.

"Dave says he wants a sausage" said Jayne.

"Nah!" mumbled Scott.

"Do you hear that, Dave?" said Jayne. "There's no sausages"

"Can you...come back later?" grunted Scott.

"What?" exclaimed Jayne. "I'm coming in"

"*Wait!*" screamed Scott.

At this point cold fear finally overcame the backlog. Scott gave himself a quick wipe with a dirty pair of pants, threw a t-shirt over the pan, and secreted it back in the corner. Not a moment too soon, as Jayne's lovely but rather stern face appeared, only to recoil, fanned frantically by Jayne's left hand.

"Pardon me while I puke" she said.

It was a cruel moment: Scott's ultimate fantasy, to be intimate in a tent with Jayne, had been realised, but only as part of the most unholy threesome.

"A dog must have got into our tent" Scott explained.

"What, and shat in it?" asked Jayne.

"Yeah, shat in my mum's saucepan, the fucker" replied Scott.

"Oh, Jesus!" cried Jayne. "That's rank! And you've just left it there?"

"Yeah, well..." began Scott, "...it's not like we're at home"

"What?" exclaimed Jayne.

"You know" blabbed Scott. "'Clear up your mess, like good bourgeois children'"

Jayne viewed him with disbelief. "Scott, it's dogshit!" she railed. "That's a fucking health hazard!"

"Ok, ok, I'll move it" replied Scott.

"I really am going to puke" said Jayne, as Scott lifted the offending pan. "A dog's shat in Scott's tent" she called back to the Alleynians.

Scott's interrogation was far from over. As he emerged from his tent with the milk pan, explanations were required as to when and how a dog could have got into a tent whose front flaps were securely tied, when Clem and Toby were just yards away. Evidently a small and ingenious animal, suggested Scott. Chihuahua maybe...Manchester terrier... or couldn't a Dandy Dinmont be trained to go down a very small pothole?

There was, however, a contradiction in this argument which played on Clem's sharp and analytical mind.

"If the dog's so small" he enquired, "how come its turd is so big?"

"There's not always a correlation" replied Scott, unconvincingly.

"They must be some correlation" replied Clem. "You can't have a turd that's bigger than the dog itself"

"Let's find the dog that did it" suggested Toby.

Clem viewed his companion with withering scorn. "I knew you shouldn't have had that early morning joint" he remarked.

"Seriously" replied Toby, "we can't have people letting their dogs do that"

"What, do you think it's going to shit in everyone else's tent?" asked Clem.

"It might do" replied Toby, "now that it's established a habit"

Jayne, still tipsy from the poteen, recognised the apparent good sense in Toby's suggestion.

"Can't be hard to find the dog that small" she mused.

"With an anus that big" added Clem.

"What about breakfast?" mumbled Dave.

"I don't think I can eat now" replied Jayne.

A new wave of depression hit Scott, mingled with a destructive anger. Just as he'd set things up so well he had wrecked them again through his own stupid inhibitions. There would be no breakfast, except for the flies, and a day of such promise was set to be yet another day of frustration and disappointment.

Into this scenario came Claus, shaking Scott's one free hand with uninhibited vigour. "Scott!" he declaimed. "I've been looking for you!"

"I've got to - " began Scott, but Claus's speech was already prepared.

"You've read the article on *In Place of Strife*?" he demanded.

"Um -"

"Why do *you* think Wilson dropped it?"

"Er -"

"Can't you see the TUC is just doing Wilson's dirty work for him?"

Scott had actually failed to read a single article of the *Morning Star* handed him by Claus and knew virtually nothing about *In Place of Strife* other than it was something to do with Barbara Castle and the unions didn't like it. *In Place of Strife,* like most matters affecting workers, did not feature in the underground press which was Scott's main source of radical education. Scott, at that moment, was only interested in his own antidote to strife, which involved everybody and in particular Claus fucking off and leaving him to dispose of his turd in the nearest bushes.

At this point an unlikely saviour appeared. Gerry approached, happily oblivious to his favourite milk pan, childish excitement lighting up his face. Scott had witnessed such an expression many times as Gerry unwrapped a new LP, but it had been conspicuously absent since they had arrived at Wootton.

"Come with me, Scott boy!" enthused Gerry. "We are *made!*"

"This is Gerry" mumbled Scott, but it was the last words he managed to Jayne as Gerry swept him away. The would-be breakfasters soon became a disorientated and disconsolate knot in the distance.

"Got your pass?" asked Gerry.

"Yeah, why?" asked Scott.

"Follow me" replied Gerry.

Gerry entered the arena through the nearest gate, but rather than follow the crowd who were racing for prime position for that day's entertainment, he then headed straight for the next gate, through which the two directly exited. As they did so they were handed two small glossy pieces of paper headed PASS OUT.

"We don't need these" remarked Scott.

"Exactly!" said Gerry. "We can sell them!" He dug into his pockets and triumphantly flourished a further four pass-outs.

"I don't want to do this" said Scott.

Gerry heaved a long-suffering sigh. "Oh, come on, Scott!" he implored.

"Why don't we just give them away?" asked Scott.

"Because people will pay for them, that's why!" railed Gerry.

"That's no reason" replied Scott.

"Good enough reason for me" responded Gerry.

"I'm just giving this to someone" insisted Scott.

"Oh, for fuck's sake, Scott" replied Gerry. "We worked to get these passes. Why should other people get in for nothing?"

"Because it should be a free festival" asserted Scott.

"Yeah, then who pays for the bands?" countered Gerry.

"We're not paying for the bands by selling these pass-outs" replied Scott.

"Look, Scott" said Gerry, laying a hand on Scott's shoulder and adopting an oh-so-reasonable tone. "People out here want to see the bands. We're helping them to get what they want, and for our trouble, we're taking a little reward. So everyone's happy. Now come along, let's get ouselves a few quid, then we can buy you some decent clothes, and maybe you might just pull that bird you fancy"

"What bird I fancy?" replied Scott.

"Word gets round, Scott" responded Gerry.

Scott was thrown. Had Clem said something? But he had confessed nothing to Clem. Was his attraction to Jayne so obvious?

"Come on mate, I'll even help you choose a t-shirt" pressed Gerry.

Scott's resolve had been weakened by Gerry's matey hand, and his friend's new line of argument had hit upon a particularly soft spot. Scott had already been eyeing up a lime-green tie-dye grandad vest in the temporary shops, wondering how well it would play with Jayne if he dressed as her twin.

Besides, Scott had to be realistic. It wasn't within his power to eliminate the division between the haves and the have-nots and turn the Isle of Wight into a free festival. To give away a couple of pass-outs would be no more than a token gesture. Was it just a terrible crime to sell them at a modest price, just enough to secure the items that might change his life forever?

"Ok, I'll sell this one" Scott concurred. "But that's it"

"Good on you, Scott" replied Gerry, giving him a wholesome pat on the back. "But if you get a crowd round you, send 'em on to me, right?"

The far side of the perimeter fence, abutting the second camping field, looked like fertile ground. Large knots of hopefuls had gathered around one area of fence which had been breached, apparently by somebody tunnelling under. Security were onto the spot, but in small numbers and with only one dog, so that a mass onslaught could potentially have led to at least a few successes. Clearly, however, the onlookers had neither the confidence or cohesion for this. Even an anarchist could recognise the need for leadership.

The situation wrecked Scott's weak resolve to become a capitalist. His immediate instinct was to become that missing leader. According to Scott's rule of thumb, anyone being barked at by an alsatian had to be in the right; to be locked out of a party, moreover, was to be a victim of an elementary injustice, whatever the reason. Faced with the reality of having to hawk his ill-gotten pass-out rather than storm the barricades, Scott's mouth dried and brain fogged.

"Anyone want a ticket?" he offered weakly.

Gerry had meanwhile adopted the air of a Class A drug dealer, moving surreptitiously through the crowd, flashing his sale item left and right, hoping to start a bidding war. Glancing back to check Scott was still with him, he was astonished to see his schoolmate deluged by urgent punters. All had assumed the ticket was going free, a presumption that Scott now found it impossible to negate. He stood helpless in a sea of demand, no idea how to resolve the situation, until one individual established herself forcibly as being of the greatest need. She did this by planting her face no more than a foot away from Scott's, her gypsy kerchief pulled tight over a pair of black eyes whose intensity liquefied Scott's timid innards.

"Can I have it for a kiss?" she asked.

There was a hint of madness in the girl's eyes, or at the very least monomania. Her face was hard but not that bad-looking, with a gap between her front teeth which according to Isaac Watts folklore indicated nymphomania. She was older, too, maybe twenty-five, or a twenty-one who'd lived hard, which seemed feasible.

"I've *got* to see Joe Cocker" the girl added, tipping her head to one side and staring unflinchingly into Scott's eyes.

Scott was stalemated. This, surely, was prostitution, a limited form maybe, but involving the exchange of sexual favours for payment all the same. Prostitution was definitely not part of the new movement.

"You can just have it" he said.

"Ok" said the girl. She removed the pass-out from Scott's hand, but kissed him all the same, fully on the lips, and in a way which brought her breasts, covered merely by a thin seersucker blouse, snugly up to his chest, if only for a few seconds.

It was a watershed moment for Scott. According to his diary it was three months and two days since he'd snogged a girl and almost six since he'd touched a breast, even through clothing. The sperm factory that was his adolescent body now went into overdrive, so that what had been a moist hope now became a coruscating imperative. Sex was a necessity, preferably with the girl in front of him but failing that the ultimate dream of Jayne or any reasonably attractive alternative including his beloved right hand.

Option A did not last long. Thrilled with her booty, seersucker girl was already en route to her encounter with the gas fitter from Sheffield whose *Delta Lady* rang out so frequently over the festival PA. Scott watched her disappearance with gloom, wondering if he had at last met the Ruby Tuesday butterfly child of popular song, that airy and slightly brainless spirit of ecstasy who would provide a man with a robust shag without troubling him the next day.

Into the vaccuum of her former presence stepped Gerry. "Did you just give that to her?" he demanded.

"What's it to you?" replied Scott.

"Christ, you did" said Gerry.

Scott felt a little surge of anger. "It was my pass out" he asserted. "You do what you want with yours, and I'll do what I want with mine"

Gerry folded his arms and viewed Scott clinically, as he had done many times before, usually before some crushing put-down.

"What are you looking at me like that for?" asked Scott.

"You're never going to be like Joe, Scott" sneered Gerry. "No matter how hard you try"

Scott was flabbergasted. "I'm not trying to be like Joe!" he protested.

Gerry smirked. "It's written all over your face, Scott" he said.

"I am not!" exclaimed Scott.

"Scott, what are you getting so worked up for?" laughed Gerry.

"Listen" said Scott, now fuming. "Why don't you go off and have your festival, and I'll have mine, and we'll see how we both get on, shall we?"

Gerry adopted a knowing expression. "So you're chickening out" he scoffed.

"Eh?" replied Scott. "What of?"

"Making the bootleg" responded Gerry.

"Actually" said Scott, "I'd forgotten all about it"

"Very convenient" replied Gerry.

"Not at all" said Scott. "I've just got other things to think about"

"Yeah, like getting to college" replied Gerry.

"What's that's got got to do with it?" demanded Scott.

"Got to be a good boy to go to college" said Gerry.

"Oh, come on" said Scott.

"You don't take drugs, you don't skive school -" began Gerry.

"I have skived school!" protested Scott.

"Oh yeah?" scoffed Gerry. "When?"

"I'm not having this discussion here" replied Scott.

"So are you making the bootleg?" pressed Gerry.

"Yes!" cried Scott.

"We'll see" replied Gerry, again with a knowing expression, this time so complacent Scott could have punched him straight in the face. To Scott's imperative to have sex by whatever means was added a second: to prove Gerry wrong no matter the cost.

Arriving back at the camping field Scott was disappointed to find only one person in the proximity of his tent: Cressida. Scott instinctively felt a pang of sympathy for this forlorn figure: after all, she was the archetypal outsider, shunned or patronised virtually from her first words to the group, primarily for the sin of being needy, or an 'emotional parasite' as Clem put it. Maybe, thought Scott, she had had a relationship with Dylan – after all, allegedly, many women could make this claim. Scott resolved to speak to her with an open mind.

"Hello" she said, in a desultory tone. She sat cross-legged, hunch-backed, her eyes distant and her top lip overhanging a lethargically open mouth. "I've got a headache" she added.

"I've got some paracetamol" replied Scott.

"It's not that kind of headache" complained Cressida.

"What kind is it?" asked Scott.

"Can I lie in your tent?" Cressida suddenly demanded.

"Um...I suppose so...haven't you got your own tent?" enquired Scott.

"My tent's got a bad vibe" replied Cressida.

Scott's eyes fell on the milk pan he had abandoned. "Mine too" he said.

"I don't sense it" replied Cressida.

"Maybe you've got a cold" said Scott.

For the first time Cressida's eyes met Scott's. She did actually have quite striking eyes, ash grey and piercing, though massively deluged in black mascara. "I haven't got a cold" she asserted.

"Yeah, you can lie in our tent if you like" said Scott, wondering if the meaningful conversation he envisaged might be more likely after Cressida had had a good lie-down.

"Thanks" said Cressida. She rolled over onto hands and knees and crawled into Scott's tent, revealing a portion of knicker from which Scott, despite the state of his libido, was inclined to avert his eyes.

Scott pondered his next move, unaware that this was about to be decided for him. Maurice Moss, following Gerry's directions, was making his way towards the circle of tents, accompanied by a small, rubbery-faced man with wild sideburns and a yo-yo which lit as it was thrown and retrieved. Catching sight of Scott, Maurice raised a fist on high and declaimed loudly:

"All hail the hero of the festival!"

After his experience with Gerry, Maurice was the last person Scott wanted to see. "Don't take the piss" he replied.

"I'm not talking about you, Scott" said Maurice. "I'm talking about me"

"Oh yeah?" replied Scott, casting an anxious glance over Maurice's peculiar companion.

"Those of us in the know" announced Maurice, "know that the Who will be playing today. It's all sorted"

"And?" replied Scott.

"And they're coming by helicopter" continued helicopter, "so everyone's going spare saying how the fuck are they going to land a helicopter backstage with all the marquees and those old biddies in their bungalow and everything"

"Don't tell me" said Scott. "You're going to pilot it"

"Meanwhile I've remembered that we had a load of

fence panels left over" continued Maurice, "so I say, 'how about making an H out of them for a target?' And Rikki Farr says, 'Maurice, you are a fucking genius! How can we ever fucking repay you?'. So I says, 'I'll have your cowboy hat, Rikki'. 'Will you fuck!' he says. Tell you man, if Dylan said he wanted that hat Rikki'd tell *him* to fuck off"

"We ought to nick it" added Maurice's companion, in a heavy accent which Scott could not place, other than it was east of Berlin.

"Yeah, fucking right, and hold it for ransom!" trilled Maurice.

"He'd go mental" said Maurice's mate.

"Yeah, and we'd say, 'you may be the son of the greatest heavyweight this country ever produced, but we've got your fucking hat and we want a grand for it!" replied Maurice.

"Yeah, and take your brother off the bill, cos we know he only got the gig cos you're the compere" added Maurice's mate.

"Oh, come on, man" replied Maurice, suddenly serious. "Gary's a good guy. He let me play his guitar"

Scott's weariness was growing. "Did you want something?" he asked.

Maurice focused all his attention on Scott. There was a challenge in his eyes. "The question is Scott" he said, "is there something *you* want?"

"Like what?" asked Scott, fearing the worst.

"This is Max" announced Maurice, finally introducing his companion. "Max can get you anything, and I mean anything"

"Hi man" said Max. He extended a hand which Scott briefly shook.

"This is a guy you should respect" declared Maurice. "He stowed away for a month to get to this country. They'd kill him if he went back to Russia"

"It's true" declared Max.

"Max was head of the underground Beatles fan club" added Maurice.

Max nodded emphatically.

"Can't you listen to the Beatles in Russia?" asked Scott.

"Are you joking?" replied Max. "Just to be found with one single would mean prison at least"

"That's ridiculous" said Scott.

"They know the power of this music" replied Max. "This music will bring down Communism"

Scott thought of saying that he was hoping it would bring down capitalism, but he didn't anticipate either a laugh or a sympathetic hearing. Judging by Max's general demeanour, belt-bags and bulging pockets, market trading was very much his game.

Sure enough, Max clarified their purpose. "Listen man" he whispered. "I've got hash, acid, Mandrax, purple hearts…"

"I'm not really, um…" began Scott.

"You're not really what?" queried Max, intense in his interrogation.

"Not really into that" replied Scott.

"Not really into what?" asked Max.

"Drugs" replied Scott.

Max laughed a little. "What, you don't take aspirin?" he asked.

"No, I don't mean - " began Scott.

"You know where Coca Cola got its name?" asked Max. "It had cocaine in it. So then it was good, but now it's bad. And now Coca Cola has caffeine in it. Man, take enough caffeine, it will fuck up your heart. No-one's heart has been fucked up by acid"

"I have had some pot" said Scott, apologetically.

"Man" said Max, "if you don't want to open up your mind, what are you doing in this place?"

Following on from Gerry's taunts, Max's challenge hit home. No matter how much he feared the consequences, Scott simply had to take the risk and let go. Having those few joints the previous evening had loosened his tongue and broken the ice with Jayne, so what might be the effect of speed or acid? Might they wrench away the effects of five years of grammar school education, make him into a part of this movement, render him instantly attractive to the festival's womenfolk?

Max seemed to sense Scott's weakening. He took out a small plastic bag from his pocket.

"You can have these for free" he said.

Max handed Scott the bag. Inside was a tangled knot of spindly dried mushrooms.

"What are they?" he asked.

"What are they!" scoffed Maurice.

"Psilocybin" said Max. "What you call magic mushrooms"

"Are they safe?" asked Scott.

Maurice adopted the air of a wordly-wise teacher. "Listen, man" he began. "People were taking these things before they invented the wheel. The ancient religions used them. They were part of the rituals. All we're doing is rediscovering them. All this is just getting back to how it used to be, before the fucking Christians moved in"

"What about bad trips?" asked Scott.

"I've done it before" replied Maurice. "As long as you're with someone who knows what they're doing, you'll be alright"

"Vitamin C stops bad trips" declared Max.

Maurice nodded. He knew this was bollocks, an urban myth, but holding a penny had once stopped his carsickness.

"Are you taking some then?" asked Scott.

"We're already on them" replied Maurice.

"Just starting to work" added Max, with a broad smile.

"See?" said Maurice. "We're all right"

"I'll give you fifty" declared Max. "That is enough to trip, but not so heavy"

"How long does it last?" asked Scott.

"A few hours" replied Max.

"You'll be straight by the time the Who arrive" added Maurice.

"On the big H" said Max, slapping Maurice's back.

"Hey, have you heard?" asked Maurice. "The Beatles are going to jam with Dylan"

"Lennon's already here" added Max. "We saw him in the VIP area"

"Do you want me to do you an omelette or something?" Maurice asked Scott.

"Can't I just eat them?" asked Scott.

"Sure" said Max. "They taste like...mushroom". He and Maurice laughed.

Max counted out Scott's portion, Scott steeled himself, then began his first psychedelic brunch.

Six

The change came slowly, almost imperceptibly. Scott and his new companions had decided to while away some time watching the incongruous spectacle of the car jousting arena, where crude paint jobs and expanded polysytrene had transformed a few old bangers into alternative gladiators, bringing some jovial warfare to the fields of peace. The three's interest in the entertainment soon waned, and the conversation turned to the universal currency of Beatledom. For Scott, like so many millions, each release of a Beatles single had been a landmark, and their sprouting facial hair was the measure of the changing times. *All You Need Is Love* announced that the new age had arrived; *Hey Jude* confirmed that the Beatles' search for enlightenment was not in vain. But the significance of these songs to Scott was nothing compared to their importance to Max, who could recount every detail of the nervous gatherings of friends in his flat to listen to John and Paul's voices calling out from that exotic land of freedom known as Liverpool.

The sight of the comedy cars smashing hell out of each other seemed even more incongruous to the soundtrack of Max's voice. Scott began to prefer the appearance of his own arms, especially now his veins had become busy motorways, the corpuscles like a multicoloured stream of taxis. How strange it was, thought Scott, that he should have developed x-ray vision just as Max was discussing the technology of converting secret recordings onto singles made from x-ray plates.

But something else was working its way into Scott's consciousness: a gradual awareness that all was not well in his guts.

"My stomach feels bad" he informed Maurice.

"It'll pass" Maurice replied.

"What is it?" asked Scott.

"Just the poison" replied Maurice.

For a moment Scott forgot what he had taken and why. "What poison?" he asked, anxiously.

"Scott, don't worry!" replied Maurice. "It'll pass"

But the seed of fear was planted in Scott's mind, and now he was aware he was in place far from normality, from which he could not escape, an animal panic began to overtake him.

"I want to get out of this" he mumbled.

Maurice and Max immediately recognised the onset of a bad trip, and not wanting to be brought down themselves, went into overdrive to pull Scott out of it. He was plied with Corona orangeade, assured the massive amounts of vitamin C this contained would neutralise the wobblies, and led from the hustle and bustle of the car jousting to the relative quiet of Palmers Road, the dirt track which led down to Wootton and the prospect of escape. Unfortunately, however, the three had barely arrived at this reassuring pathway when two new arrivals appeared around the corner, filled with the zeal of the almighty and a mission to save the fallen. Now it was Max's turn to feel panicky, while Scott, warmed by his Corona, was merely amused.

"Penguins!" he trilled.

"That's not penguins" murmured Max, crossing himself. "That's nuns"

"I'm seeing witches" said Maurice.

"I'm telling you, it's nuns!" exclaimed Max.

Maurice readjusted his sights. "What are they doing here?" he asked.

"Maybe one of them's the Singing Nun" replied Scott.

"Don't let them talk to me" said Max.

The three tripping young men were, however, directly in the sights of the holy sisters, though it was Scott who particularly attracted them, due to his obvious youth and uncertainty. The elder of the two nuns approached him with a patient smile.

"Does your mother know you're here, young man?" she asked, softly.

Scott was unable to reply, not because he did not know the answer, but because his interrogator, who had certainly been a nun a few moments before, had resolved herself once more into a penguin, a talking penguin, from the same stable maybe as the pushmi-pullyu, the gub-gub and the chee-chee. Was it possible, moreover, that Scott actually *was* Doctor Doolittle? He knew for a fact that the person alongside him was called Maurice, and wasn't that the name of his great friend, the cat's meat man?

It was Maurice who replied to the nun. "Does your mother know you're here?" he asked.

The elder nun scrutinised Maurice before turning to her younger accomplice. "He's high" she noted.

"Correct" replied Maurice.

The elder nun readdressed herself to Scott. "I was asking if your mother knows you are here" she pronounced.

"And I was asking if your mother knows you're here" repeated Maurice.

The elder nun was entirely unfazed. "All our ministrations are approved by our mother superior" she asserted.

"Mother superior?" scoffed Maurice. "Does that make you Daughter Inferior?"

There was a long pause. "Have you considered why you need these drugs?" asked the nun.

"You've got a drug" replied Maurice. "It's called Jesus. At least my drugs don't start wars"

Maurice's words struck Scott as being of great profundity, profundity that had obviously been liberated by whatever it was they had taken, as Maurice still faithfully attended religious assembly at school, whereas Scott had faced all manner of shit for refusing to do so, including being consigned to a small depressing room to make notes on a book of Greek ethical philosophy. Was it possible that Isaac Watts had sent these creatures to the festival to prevent his further degeneration? Or was their arrival connected to Gerry's claim that Butterhorn were bigger than Jesus, or (to supply the full quote from the Locks Heath Herald, so often overlooked by historians), "bigger than Jesus in Warsash"?

The Beatles, of course, had paid the full price for Lennon's own observation about their popularity, that joyfully dry Liverpudlianism which so many Americans failed to get. It was some achievement to have great piles of their records burning in the States while Brezhnev and friends were hunting them down with equal fervour on the other side of the Iron Curtain: a sure sign, in Scott's eyes, that they must have been doing something right.

For the moment, however, Scott was not up to joining in with Maurice's philosophical debate, even though the other end of the pushmi-pullyu was now advising him in a slightly friendlier manner of her own encounter with Jesus and the search for the reality of a living God which had brought her to this place and to young people like him seeking enlightenment just as she had once done. Scott was in the world beyond words, noting how this end of the pushmi-pullyu was quite tolerably attractive, and vaguely wondering if by taking a few drugs herself she might throw off the garments of sexual shame and reunite flesh and spirit as per the soft porn cliché.

Suddenly, as if in a Cecil B. De Mille epic, the voice of God thundered from the skies, announcing the imminent arrival of the Edgar Broughton Band.

"Rikki!" cried Maurice, delightedly.

"Let's go now" declared Max, who had borne the whole encounter with the nuns as if backed against a wall by men with knives.

Maurice, however, had been doubly energised by hearing the voice of his supposed great friend. Sensing the odds in his favour against the nuns, roughly a hundred thousand to two, his voice took on more of a taunting air. "Coming to see Edgar Broughton, ladies" he enquired, "or is that the devil's music?"

"You would know better than me" replied the elder nun.

"That's right" crowed Maurice. "See, I'm a music fan, and this is a music festival, so why don't you get back to doing what you normally do, like torturing schoolgirls?"

Right or wrong, the vision of schoolgirls tortured by a pushmi-pullyu caused Scott to break down into fits of helpless laughter, in which he was soon joined by Maurice, till the two of them were lost in a world of hilarity painful in its intensity.

"May God forgive you" replied the nun, with feeling, gathering her accomplice and marching smartly off in the direction of the St John's ambulance tent. Their dramatic exit only added to Scott and Maurice's helplessness, till Scott's diaphragm was so tight he feared he would stop breathing altogether.

"You should not have said those things" commented Max.

Maurice's giggles subsided just enough to speak. "Don't bring us down, man" he replied.

"Don't let me down!" warbled Scott, attempting to cover the recent Beatles hit, but sounding so woeful his effort set both off again in shuddering mirth, sufficient to send Max hastening towards the arena gate. This sight sobered Maurice immediately: under the influence of the mushrooms, the desire to flock together was paramount, especially when one of the company was your passport to credibility.

In sober times Scott was not the greatest fan of the Edgar Broughton band, with their plodding heavy blues and pantomime villain vocals, but suddenly, as they exploded into action over the massive PA, it was a new band Scott heard, blood-stirringly raw, impossibly exciting. This was a sound to blow that pushmi-pullyu right back to the funny farm.

Max had reached the queue waiting to get through the gate. Maurice joined him with a friendly arm around the shoulder. "Sos, mate" he said. "Didn't mean to freak you out"

"There are powers you shouldn't mess with" replied Max.

Max said this with great weight, but for Scott this was entirely subverted by the fact Max's head was held in two great hairy hands (formerly sideburns) which lent him the appearance of someone in trauma, not unlike the figure in Munch's *The Scream*. Hardly over his last fit of giggles, Scott burst out laughing once again, bringing Maurice down with him, so that the deadly serious Max now began to suffer serious paranoia.

"What is so funny?" he demanded.

Scott was incapable of replying and Maurice had to admit he didn't know, but the more offended Max looked, the more hilarious he became, and the fact that Scott and Maurice knew they shouldn't be laughing only made it worse.

"Stop fucking laughing!" demanded Max.

The trip was going in a seriously bad direction, and no-one seemed to have any control over it.

"Can you stop looking so serious?" pleaded Scott.

"Not when you're taking the piss out of me!" replied Max. There was now a clear threat of violence in the air and onlookers were starting to intervene with pleas for peace which only seemed to wind Max up more.

"Don't talk about peace to me!" he cried. "Haven't you seen the fucking warships over there?" Max gestured vaguely in the direction of the stage, confusing everybody.

"It's ok, guys, he's tripping" explained Maurice, who had stopped laughing.

"Portsmouth!" cried Max, gesturing more forcefully. "I'm talking about Portsmouth!"

"Pompey!" enthused one of the crowd.

"Do you think they're all going to turn into butterflies after Dylan has come?" asked Max. "No, there is going to be war, so fucking wake up!"

Max's audience resumed their queueing. He wasn't the first person to go off his head at this event. There was a tent for people like him in the field behind.

Another person, however, had begun to take a keen interest in the three trippers. Up ahead in the ticket booth, Lewis Croker stood grim-faced with a testing screwdriver in one hand and a spotlight bulb in the other. The electrician's son was not happy. He had worked long hours for a week, done everything asked of him to a professional standard, and was now ready to dip into his own supply of recreational drugs and flake out to the music. It did not amuse him to have further work to do because Matt White had trusted a mouthy idiot to know what he was doing, particularly a mouthy idiot from the school every other school in Southampton hated.

Scott could not quite place the long-armed razor-eyed youth approaching, but rightly sensed that he, like the grey ships over the Solent, was not intent on peace.

"Where's your mate today?" snapped Lewis.

Scott checked the screwdriver and everything fell into place. "Gerry's not really my mate" he replied.

"Bollocks" replied Lewis. "You brought him, and he fucked up, so you can put it right"

Max smiled at Scott. "So now it's your turn" he remarked.

Lewis held out a toiletry bag containing screwdriver, wire cutters, pliers and a Stanley knife, which to Scott seemed like a bag of bizarre and inedible sweets. "I've just fixed the light here" he said, "now you get down to the next gate and fix that one. Thanks to your mate they had no light last night"

"I don't know what to do" pleaded Scott.

"Now's your time to learn" replied Lewis.

"But what do I do?" repeated Scott.

"Check. The. Connections" replied Lewis, spelling it out with ill-disguised contempt for his hapless audience.

"I want to see this band" implored Scott.

"Tough" replied Lewis.

"I'll do it later" Scott pleaded.

"No you won't" asserted Lewis.

Maurice, fresh from his victorious encounter with the nuns, took it upon himself to save the situation. "You can't tell Scott what to do" he asserted. "He's not your employee"

Lewis viewed this new challenge clinically. "What's that on his pass?" he asked.

Scott examined the arena pass in his hand. He could read it, after a fashion, but the letters would keep jumping up and reassembling themselves.

"Electrician" Lewis reminded him.

Neither Scott nor Maurice could disagree.

"If he's not an electrician" asserted Lewis, "I'll have that pass"

Checkmate.

"I'll do it later" repeated Scott.

Lewis pressed the toiletry bag into Lewis's hand with a little more force than necessary, enough to register a hint of malice, especially to a rasping soundtrack of Edgar Broughton. "Get on with it, sunshine" he commanded.

"Ok, man, ok" said Max, who was now keen to get rid of the icy eyes and get the trip back on track. "We'll do it together" he said to Scott.

Scott buzzed inwardly. It was good to feel they were one again. The trippers banded into a tight pack and headed confidently up the dirt track towards the second gate: the idea that the three together could achieve what none could manage individually was a compelling one. Reaching the queue for the gate, they formed a huddle to discuss tactics.

"Scott" declared Maurice, removing the screwdriver from the toiletry bag, "this tool is your responsibility. Any time we need to use it, it's your job"

Scott took the screwdriver. Suddenly his confidence melted. "I can't do this" he muttered.

"Of course you can" Max assured him. "All you need is to be the boss of the electricity. It's like a horse. If it knows you're the boss, it is no trouble"

"That is so fucking true" chimed Maurice. "You take the wire-cutters, Max"

"Then you have the pliers *and* the knife" commented Max.

"I'm ok with that" Maurice assured him. "Hold on, there's something else in here" He rummaged in the bag and produced a roll of insulating tape. "You take that, Scott" he ordered.

Scott took the tape. The memory of the event in the Victory Hall returned. Tape was dangerous.

"Let's go to work" said Max. He made his way up the queue, apologies mixed with stern assurances as to the importance of their purpose. "We've come to fix the electrics" he informed the man in the ticket booth.

"All of you?" asked the man. The ticket booth was not much larger than a telephone kiosk.

"We're a team" Maurice advised him.

The ticket man was not happy, but made way for the trio to squeeze in behind him and appraise the situation. A spotlight was screwed to the side of the kiosk, from which a wire descended into a connector, inexpertly wrapped in tape, then on to a plug fitted into a socket, from which another wire rose to a junction with the mains. It was an impossibly complex arrangement, obviously requiring far more skill than the team had anticipated. For Scott the picture was further complicated by the fact he could see the stream of electrons, brilliant silver, and sense their urgent desire to penetrate the highway of corpuscles and seize his heart.

"I don't think we should be doing this" he suggested.

"They said that to Dylan" commented Max.

"Turning your back on electricity" remarked Maurice, "is turning your back on the future"

As if to confirm Maurice's wisdom, Edgar Broughton burst into life again. What was that power but the power of the devil-god electricity?

Scott gazed in fear and awe at the thin spotlight lead, seeing now a tributary of a titanic river, so immense, so coruscating it could either create a new world or destroy history. In point of fact, the stage electrics were none of Croker's responsibility, on a completely different circuit to the perimeter and marquees, but even had he known this, Scott would still have been convinced all electricity was One, a force to be worshipped, not poked with screwdrivers.

"We've got to check the connections" pronounced Maurice, remembering Lewis's instructions.

"That's a connection" asserted Max, indicating the tape-wound connector beneath the spotlight.

"Tape" said Maurice. "That's your job, Scott"

Scott viewed Gerry's crude handiwork, heart pumping, guts rediscovering their former disorder. "What do I do?" he whimpered.

"It's very easy" Max assured him. "Just unwind the tape and see if the wires are out"

Scott picked at the end of the tape without conviction. Suddenly there was a surge, a surge of memory of the Victory Hall. "No!" he cried. "It's alive!"

The ticket office man looked back over his shoulder anxiously. Maurice dug a fist into Scott's ribs and urged him to hush.

"We've got to take the plug out" Scott implored.

Maurice and Max looked down at the plug in question, both faintly amazed that Scott had proved to be the one with the practical expertise.

"He's right" said Max.

"You do it, Max" said Maurice.

Max reached down for the plug. But Scott had had a change of heart. "No!" he cried. "Don't do it!" The panic on his face baffled his companions but made absolute sense to Scott. If they pulled that plug, Edgar Broughton would be instantly silenced, the burgers would freeze on their griddles and darkness would reign in the toilet tent.

"Scott's just freaking out" said Maurice, an observation confirmed by his schoolmate's mad scramble to get out of the booth and as far away as possible from the situation. Obeying the classic animal rule of fight or flight, Scott pelted across the arena, failing completely to note Jayne and Dave at the rear of the audience, stopping only when the crowd was too thick to allow futher ingress.

Too late, Scott realised there was no security here. Instinctively he dug into his pocket, for a decade the home of the half crown his dad had given him in the event of emergencies. Instead of that weighty and comforting coin, however, he found a small slip of card featuring a bizarre art deco toad man in evening wear, alongside which was scrawled ELECTRICIANS. As the patterns around the toad man flashed gold and red like a neon sign, Scott wracked his brains to understand the card's meaning, before turning it to find another figure, a gruesome tiger man, above the legend "Godshill ISLE OF WIGHT", the number 3490/B, and the scrawled words NON PRESS.

Scott's bafflement grew. The tiger man grasped his lapel and stared with dreadful ferocity, mouth agape, eyes aflame. What could this have to do with Godshill, that benign tourist trap of pubs and gift shops, the Old Smithy and the model village? Were those eyes telling Scott something about Godshill that the casual tourist would not notice? Was Godshill the key to something much greater, a portal into an unseen universe behind the clematis, the miniature churches and the strawberry ices?

Scott's dad had a book about Godshill. J.B.Priestley. He was a socialist. Did that link in somehow?

Scott fished into his other pocket and brought out his arena pass. That, too, had ELECTRICIANS scrawled on it. The writing matched. The other card had to be some kind of pass. Was there another festival in Godshill?

Yes! That was it! There was another festival, a festival Matt White had talked about, but that had started the the year before, and surely could not still be going on, unless watching Isle of Wight festivals was like painting the Forth bridge, a Herculean labour.

The thought of Matt White brought back another of their conversations, and with sudden certainty Scott realised that this ticket, whatever it might look like, was actually his pass to that picket-fenced sanctuary known as the VIP area. Immediately Scott began pressing on, hurdling irritated bodies on his way to that place of ultimate security. How could he have questioned the right of the rich and famous to have such a place? Every creature on God's earth sought a safe refuge.

Scott was right about the ticket. The security man took one glance and ushered him through. There were numerous empty chairs in the enclave; Scott sat half way back, safe enough from the crowd behind but not so near he could see the whites of Edgar Broughton's eyes. Up this close, the stacks of WEM speakers sent out a level of volume that was almost like a physical assault. Scott's innards boiled as he desperately tried to control his head and the furry tennis ball that had become lodged in his throat.

Suddenly, as if from nowhere, there was a naked woman. She had somehow managed to get herself right in front of the candy-striped stage and was giving herself to the music with total abandon.

Scott's tennis ball dissolved as he became transfixed by the spectacle before him. Suddenly the festival had a totem, a vanguard, stripped of all defence. This was true commitment to the cause, but how great the risk! The woman had sacrificed herself. She was a human sacrifice to the press pack who flocked round her like gulls at a stranded fish. As the cameras clicked and popped around him, Scott began to feel afraid for her, and then for himself. There were wasps in the beehive. How had this been allowed? What exactly was this festival, where society's freaks and outsiders were invited into this arena, this pen, then their actions observed, recorded, beamed to their enemies?

Scott's eyes shot to the fence. At that moment he could neither see nor remember any exits. Now a new panic took hold, more intense than its predecessors, terrifying and inescapable. Blindly Scott fought his way out of the VIP area, just as security enveloped the naked woman, oblivious to her scream of "I want to be free!" Scott surely would be next, if he did not run, except running was impossible over prostrate people, many of whom remembered him stumbling through them in the other direction and were not filled with great feelings of peace and love towards him. That did not matter now to Scott, however. Somehow he had to get out of this place, this hideous laboratory, this psychedelic Auschwitz. But that meant getting past security and the dogs, and Scott feared dogs as much as whatever fate awaited him if he stayed in the arena. No wonder his appearance was so desperate, no wonder everybody was viewing him with such suspicion and hostility, all the more so when the tears bubbled from his eyes and the whining began, noises he hadn't heard since he was a baby, nature noises, uncontrolled, beyond self-consciousness.

And then, above the sound of his own cries and the pitiless bark of Edgar Broughton, Scott heard someone calling his name. He turned to see Jayne. It was a miracle beyond his wildest imaginings.

"Are you all right?" she asked.

"I want to get out" replied Scott, making no attempt to hide his tears.

"What are you on?" asked Jayne.

"Mushrooms" replied Scott.

"How many?" asked Jayne.

"Forty" replied Scott.

"That's not many" said Jayne.

"Can you help me get out?" repeated Scott.

"Come on" said Jayne. She took him by the arm and he followed dutifully. The dogs stayed back, the guards melted away, and miraculously they escaped into another dimension, remarkably similar to that place where the nuns had been, but infinitely cooler and greener. They walked a little way around the perimeter, then leant on a fence overlooking the improvised car park, which seemed magically well-organised to Scott, cars fanning out in neat lines, only interrupted by patches of misplaced tents. It was good to see order: it calmed him.

"I want to get out of this" said Scott.

"This festival?" asked Jayne.

"This trip" replied Scott.

"You'e ok now" Jayne assured him. "Just go with it"

"What does that mean?" enquired Scott.

"Don't try to be be normal" counselled Jayne.

"I'm never normal" replied Scott.

Jayne was inclined to dispute this, but left it. Her eye had been caught by a building in the middle distance. "What's that place over there?" she asked.

"Which one?" asked Scott.

"There" said Jayne, pointing in the direction of Cowes. "Looks kind of Italian"

Scott followed Jayne's pointing finger, and was amazed to recognise the distant building she indicated. "Fuck me" he said. "That's Osborne House"

"Wasn't that where Queen Victoria lived?" asked Jayne.

"Better than that" said Scott. "It's where she died".

Jayne laughed.

"Not a royalist?" asked Scott.

Jayne's face twisted in distaste. "Am I fuck" she replied.

"Didn't think so" said Scott.

"Are you?" asked Jayne.

"They have their uses" replied Scott.

"Such as?" asked Jayne.

"Shooting practice" replied Scott.

Jayne laughed again. "That's fucking weird" she said. "This all happening here, when you think what happened there"

"Wonder what she'd make of the festival?" asked Scott.

"She'd probably be in the foam, shagging with Albert" laughed Jayne.

"Yeah, how many kids did they have?" asked Scott.

"Fucking hundreds" replied Jayne.

"Couldn't leave him alone" said Scott.

"Hypocrite" said Jayne.

They fell to silence, Jayne studying the peculiarities of the building, Scott remembering his visit there as a ten-year-old: the long austere corridors, Albert's peculiar bath, Victoria's obsessive collection of Indian faces, the total perversity of it all, next to which his rollercoaster drugs trip seemed almost mundane. Though scarcely political, the ten-year-old Scott was drawn obsessively to the table-deckers' quarters, the dingy site of their drudgery etching itself massively into his consciousness. He did not need to read a word of political theory to know that he was an egalitarian. How could anyone with a working heart not be an egalitarian? Everything else was bullshit.

"Why did you come here?" he suddenly asked.

Jayne broke from her reverie. "Why d'you think?" she replied. "Dylan"

"Are you a big fan?" asked Scott.

"Not particularly" replied Jayne.

"You just said you came here for him" said Scott.

"It's *Dylan*" repeated Jayne. "He's a legend"

"He is, like, the most famous man in the world, isn't he?" concurred Scott.

Jayne doubted this, but let it pass. "I can't believe I'm actually going to see Dylan" she said.

"If he turns up" said Scott.

"What, do you think he might not turn up?" asked Jayne, with a sudden frown.

"He lives in Woodstock, and he never played there" said Scott.

"He lives in Woodstock?" replied Jayne. "I never knew that"

"I don't think he wants people to know it" replied Scott.

"He's got kids now, hasn't he?" said Jayne.

"I think so, yeah" replied Scott.

"He's protecting them" said Jayne.

"I wonder what he's like as a dad?" asked Scott.

"Probably do this, do that" said Jayne.

"I don't think so" replied Scott.

"Probably gets his wife to do everything" said Jayne.

Jayne's cynicism did not derive from a bad experience of her own dad. Far from it. She liked him, on those rare occasions she saw him. Even at eighteen, however, she had felt the controlling hand of more than one weed-smoking, oh-so-liberated boyfriend. That was one reason she chose to spend her time with Dave and the others in their Regents Park squat. They were fantasists, wasters, but they let her be herself.

"Is this a normal conversation?" Scott suddenly asked.

"It's just talk" replied Jayne

"I'm trying not to be normal" said Scott.

Jayne grinned. "You're so straight!" she laughed.

"I don't think so" said Scott.

"I do" replied Jayne.

Scott bristled. Yes, he came from a suburban cul-de-sac, he had the full set of parents, but one of them regularly used him as a verbal and physical punchbag, and besides, he couldn't be part of the mainstream if he tried. For Jayne, however, normality was finding a brown house snake coiled beneath her bed, making a den and finding it inhabited by a family of nomads, being told by her brother that he may have to kill her one day. Normality was a paranoid mother, obsessed by body hair, unable to face the other wives in the officers' mess. Normality was living with that mother in silence after that mother opened Jayne's mail, found a lump of dope, and got her boyfriend sent down for three years.

"I could live in a squat if I wanted to" said Scott.

"Go on then" said Jayne.

"I don't want to" replied Scott.

"Don't knock it till you've tried it" said Jayne.

The delight and relief at finding Jayne, the sense of strength and security Scott felt in her presence, was beginning to give way to the insecurity she also fostered. Back with a wallop came Scott's abiding obsession, the nature of Jayne's relationship with Dave. Well, he had stood in his undies beside her and now cried in front of her: it seemed a small step to pop the big question.

"Are you going out with Dave?" he asked.

Jayne's manner changed. The drawbridge came down. "Why are you asking that?" she countered.

"I'm interested in people" replied Scott. It was a ridiculous thing to say, but the mushrooms were still in charge, and despite the profession of ancient peoples, they were not conferring wisdom.

"I don't want to discuss it" said Jayne.

"Why not?" asked Scott.

"Why are you interrogating me?" countered Jayne.

"I'm just interested in what it is about him that interests you" said Scott.

"Ok" said Jayne. "He's a brilliant guy. He saved my life. Is that enough?"

"He doesn't strike me as brilliant" said Scott.

"Shows what you know" replied Jayne. "He's got a double first from Cambridge"

Scott took this information like a body blow, but had lost too much control to let it lie. "I'm not even putting down for Cambridge" he declared. "I'll probably go to Sussex or East Anglia"

"Good for you" said Jayne, clearly wearying of the conversation.

"Cambridge is all about snobbery" pronounced Scott.

"Dave isn't a snob" countered Jayne.

"He went there" replied Scott.

"He's still not a snob" said Jayne.

"They don't even do sociology" replied Scott, scathingly.

Jayne sighed, eyes seeking an escape route. "I'm going back to the music" she declared.

"See you" said Scott.

"Enjoy the rest of your trip" replied Jayne.

"I think I've come down" said Scott.

"Yeah" said Jayne. "You've brought me down with you"

As soon as Jayne disappeared, Scott realised that he was not quite as sober as he had thought. The terrors had gone, but an animal appetite remained, fed by the frustration of his unrequited desire for Jayne. An unhealthy urge had sprung in him, to exact a kind of revenge for the mess she had created. He saw his sperms as electrons: dammed up they gave off red heat, dammed up further they gave off blinding light, a light that led him inexorably in the direction of his tent and the sad and alienated girl within.

No parents...no teachers...no twitching curtains...

Scott's steps grew more urgent. In his mind was his most extreme sexual liaison to date, a girl called Maxine Ashe, regarded as a scrubber by schoolmates but in Scott's experience perfectly warm and welcoming, especially with his eager teenage mouth plunging from one nipple to the other with furious enthusiasm. It was the first time Scott had done this, it was impossibly exciting, and within minutes a wondrous warm swim filled his body, followed by a luscious issue into his pants, succeeded by a bleak and sudden guilt unhelped by the fact that his mum was in the next room ironing. Poor Maxine had no idea why she was so suddenly and irascibly ejected and Scott never sought her company again.

Cressida, similarly, was unlikely to trouble Scott after the weekend. She lay exactly as he had left her, on her back, one hand against her forehead. For a brief second the image of a slaughtered Sharon Tate jumped into Scott's head, instantly dismissed.

"How's the headache?" he asked, tentatively progressing into the tent.

"A bit better, thank you" replied Cressida, in a small, girlish voice.

Scott sighed wearily. "I'm shagged" he said. "I think I'll have a lie down"

Cressida made no reply.

Scott lay down alongside her.

Cressida's eyes opened.

Scott lay a tentative hand on Cressida's side.

Cressida did not respond.

Slowly, Scott moved the hand upwards onto Cressida's breast.

Cressida's eyes met Scott's. Dolly eyes, mascara heavy, conveying no particular message. Was she a dolly bird? Was this what a dolly bird was? Cressida...sounded like a cross between Cindy and Tressy...her hair grew, at least when you turned that key in her bank and yanked the stuff out.

Scott undid a button on Cressida's top.

"I've got my period" intoned Cressida.

Scott froze. Unsure in any case where he was going, at least he could now rule out sexual intercourse.

"I could take out my tammy" she added.

Tammy...was that another doll? One that stood by her man, or filed for D.I.V.O.R.C.E? Scott searched Cressida's face for clues.

"I. Could. Take. Out. My. Tampax" she clarified.

Horror of horrors! Take out her tampax? What, there, in front of him? And then what? Carry on as if all was sweetness and light? This was no dolly bird, this was a jezebel of unspeakable depravity, sullying even the name of the saintly Tom Paxton in Scott's drug-addled mind, till all he could think was Tampax Town, Tampax Town, move over Port Sunlight and Bournville!

Scott took his hand away.

"What's the matter?" asked Cressida.

"I'm tired" replied Scott.

Cressida frowned. "You're frustrating me now" she said. She rose onto her elbows, arched her back and pulled down her knickers.

"No, don't do that" said Scott.

Cressida remained as she was, flat on her back, knickers around ankles, showing a dark thatch of pubic hair which to Scott at that moment seemed like something from the *Outer Limits*. To Scott's dismay, Cressida's hand now snaked into this alien area.

"What are you doing?" asked Scott.

"Taking out my tammy" replied Cressida.

"Jesus, no, please don't" cried Scott.

"It didn't bother Dylan" replied Cressida.

"You never slept with Dylan" scoffed Scott.

"He was a real gentleman" asserted Cressida.

"Why?" replied Scott. "Cos he slept with you when you had a period?"

"My period's nearly finished" announced Cressida. "Look"

"No thank you" blurted Scott.

"It's nothing to be ashamed of" said Cressida.

"I don't want to see your tampon!" cried Scott.

"Are you a Christian?" asked Cressida.

"No!" replied Scott.

Cressida came up onto her elbow and looked Scott in the face. "You're not very experienced, are you?" she scoffed.

Scott could not hide the shock he felt at such directness from a girl, shock which gave way to anger and a fresh awareness of being somewhere he could do or say anything, especially to Cressida, the girl from nowhere who claimed to have shagged Dylan in the back of a van.

"Maybe I don't want to get VD" he replied.

"I beg your pardon?" said Cressida.

"You've slept with a lot of people" replied Scott. "You said it yourself"

"It's called free love!" countered Cressida.

"That's just an excuse to have sex whenever you feel like it" said Scott.

"Why shouldn't you have sex whenever you feel like it?" replied Cressida.

"Not everyone you meet" said Scott.

"I don't have sex with everyone I meet" Cressida fumed.

"You were going to have sex with me" replied Scott.

"Yes, because I thought we'd made a connection!" railed Cressida.

"Free love could refer to platonic love" asserted Scott, wracking his brains for an exact quote from that book of Greek philosophy Isaac Watts had foisted on him.

Cressida shook her head and pulled her knickers back up. "I'm getting my headache back" she complained.

Scott stalled. The full import of the encounter was beginning to dawn on him. "I'm on a mushroom trip" he declared. "Can we pretend this hasn't happened?"

"Pretend what hasn't happened?" asked Cressida.

"This thing between us" replied Scott.

"There's nothing between us" declared Cressida.

"Exactly" said Scott, "so let's just keep quiet about it"

"Can you get me a backstage pass?" replied Cressida.

Scott's discomfort grew. Miraculously he had managed to empower the most powerless member of their impromptu social circle. "I've only got one" he pleaded.

"Give me that then" replied Cressida.

"I might have work to do" asserted Scott.

"Not tomorrow night" replied Cressida. "Not when Dylan's here"

Scott considered his position. "I'm taping the show" he replied, indicating the tape recorder in the rear corner of the tent.

Cressida's face fell to well-practised defeat. She began to gather her clothes and Scott left the tent, hoping against hope he'd avoid Cressida for the rest of the weekend. He'd done enough damage for one day; traumatising Dylan and sabotaging the entire festival was for another.

SEVEN

Every night in London's West End rows of well-off people in evening attire sat opposite a line of completely naked people, the most famous of whom had been photographed by a tight-trousered toff and turned into a tribal love-rock icon. Described by Vogue as the prettiest golliwog in London, Marsha Hunt was more famous for her attitude and her afro than her music, but her appearance on the Woodside Bay stage was almost as eagerly anticipated as Dylan's. After the unexpected hors d'oeuvres dished up by Edgar Broughton's bare fan, the press men hummed in anticipation of further titillation, and Marsha did not disappoint.

The boys from Dulwich College had never seen anything like it, though unsurprisingly they had different takes on the mid-afternoon entertainment. Returning to the tent camp for a civilized cup of tea, Toby and Clem bickered like an old married couple.

"Hilarious" said Clem. "The whole thing was a total piss-take"

"Pure exploitation" responded Toby.

Scott, who lay in a post-mushroom daze, aching from drained adrenaline, still not could resist seeking all the details.

"She wore black leather hotpants and a black vest" explained Toby, "and she was using the microphone as a dildo"

"Really, Toby?" queried Clem. "I never noticed that"

"If I'd wanted to see that kind of thing I'd have gone to Soho" said Toby.

"It's a rock festival" said Clem. "She's a rock singer"

"I'd hardly call her a singer at all" said Toby.

"She can't have been that bad" said Clem. "You couldn't take your eyes off her"

"I don't deny she's attractive" said Toby.

"The press have built her up as this tribal love goddess" declared Clem, "so she's playing up to it"

"Just as I said" countered Toby. "They're exploiting her, and she's encouraging it"

"Maybe you're against sexual liberation" noted Clem.

"That is not sexual liberation!" protested Toby.

"Define sexual liberation" challenged Clem.

Toby dropped teabags into the now boiling water and considered. "Sexual liberation" he declared, "is removing exploitation from the area of physical relationships, including the exploitation of women in marriage"

"Marsha Hunt isn't married" noted Clem.

Toby ignored this. "In fact" he declared, "we must supercede the two-person relationship altogether"

"Is that what Castaneda says?" scoffed Clem.

"Wilhelm Reich, actually" replied Toby.

"Another nutter" said Clem.

Toby shook his head emphatically and pointed at Clem with a teaspoon. "You should be more open-minded" he asserted.

Scott, unable to comment on Marsha Hunt's appearance, now saw a point of entry into the conversation. "Didn't Wilhelm Reich invent orgone boxes?" he asked, vaguely remembering an article from Oz or some other underground magazine.

"Yes, well, that side of his thinking was a bit eccentric, I admit" replied Toby. "But you should read *The Invasion of Compulsory Sex-Morality*. It makes a lot of sense"

"Is that the one about shagging your family?" asked Clem.

"Like I said, you should have an open mind, Clem" replied Toby.

"If that means shagging my dad, no thanks" scoffed Clem.

"There are communes based on Reich's philosophy" declared Toby, "and from what I've heard, they work very well"

"From what you've heard" repeated Clem, cynically.

"There are no restrictions on sexual expression" asserted Toby.

"Sounds like Marsha Hunt" quipped Clem.

"It is *nothing* like Marsha Hunt" retorted Toby. "People express themselves within a supportive environment, and sexual display is not just titillation, it is the prelude to healthy sexual activity"

"Shagging" quipped Clem.

"Lovemaking" countered Toby. "As opposed, for example, to marital rape"

"Eh?" responded Clem.

"Or do you deny that exists?" challenged Toby.

Clem was silent for a moment. He knew he was at a disadvantage in this conversation, being a virgin and considerably less attractive to women than Toby, despite the idiotic things his schoolfriend was inclined to say. He knew also that his comfortable home in Bromley, with his chronically inhibited parents, gave him a limited view of the wider world – not that Toby's Croydon mansion was any different. A further problem with the argument was that Clem had read Engels and understood perfectly well the link between the family, sexual morality and the accumulation of profit. Free love, moreover, might well increase his own chances in what he perceived to be a brutally competitive market for sex.

The possibility of consensus was, however, quickly killed off by Toby's next gambit:

"Personally" he declared, "I could happily sleep with anybody"

Clem spluttered with laughter. "But Toby," he enquired, "why would you *want* to sleep with anybody?"

"It's a nice thing to do" replied Toby.

"Would you sleep with Cressida?" asked Clem.

Scott winced inwardly.

"Why not?" replied Toby. "And Wendy. And Janet"

"Who's Janet?" asked Clem.

"Isn't that her name?" asked Toby.

Scott felt his bowels tighten. He knew what was coming.

"Do you mean Jayne?" asked Clem.

"Jayne, that's it" replied Toby.

A sudden loathing for Toby overwhelmed Scott. As if Jayne would sleep with an airy-fairy public schoolboy like him! Didn't he realise she was grounded, couldn't he see there wasn't the smallest iota of chemistry between them, or didn't chemistry matter when you had read Wilhelm Reich?

"Is she coming tonight?" asked Clem.

"I think so" replied Toby.

"What's happening tonight?" asked Scott, anxiously.

"We're having a bonfire" replied Toby.

"Are we?" asked Scott.

"Toby was in the boy scouts" explained Clem.

"We'll need a bonnie if it's as cold as last night" declared Toby.

"Is the jam session on?" asked Clem.

"Sure" replied Toby. "Javier's bringing his guitar"

"Who's Javier?" asked Scott, anxiety growing.

"An Argentinian guy we met" declared Toby.

"Great guy" announced Clem, authoritatively.

"This is the real festival" asserted Toby. "Right here"

It was a festival which was spinning further and further away from the world that Scott knew and the boundaries within which he felt safe to operate. Isaac Watts had instilled a keen awareness of boundaries, and Scott had once been selected as one of the virgin firsties to receive a token thrashing at the annual Beating of the Bounds ceremony. The original aim of the ritual was to ensure the boys never forgot those limits, the modern aim to reassure parents that the school had history and was peculiar enough to rank with the likes of Eton and Winchester. It was painless, yet Scott never forgot the decorous touch of the headmaster's cane. It seemed to signify that all the school's authority was part of a game, that no-one really believed any of this tosh, and that it would soon be superceded by something altogether more sensible.

Maurice Moss had missed the Beating of the Bounds ceremony, having failed to return to school that afternoon after a knee-weakening session with Ackermann's wanking club. He was, however, keen to involve Scott in a ritual of his own choosing, and was at that moment making his way round the perimeter fence to that effect.

"Rayner!" he cried, reverting to the form of address with which Scott was most familiar.

Scott disconsolately faced the music.

"What the hell happened to you?" enquired Maurice.

"Don't make a big thing of it" growled Scott, hoping the Alleynians weren't paying attention. "I've had a bad experience of electricity"

"Max said it was the funniest thing he'd ever seen" announced Maurice.

Scott doubted this, but said that he was glad he had amused them.

"We never needed you anyway" declared Maurice.

"You fixed it?" said Scott.

Maurice winked. "Didn't even need to" he replied. "Lewis came back to check on us and Max bought him off with a handful of mandies"

"He did it" said Scott.

"Yeah, and now he's going to do you" replied Maurice. "He wants your arena pass, your VIP pass, and your backstage pass. Speaking of which…" Maurice opened his address to Clem and Toby. "…they're on their way!"

"Who?" said Toby.

"Right" replied Maurice.

"Eh?" said Toby.

"The Who!" replied Maurice.

"Oh" said Toby.

Maurice reprised his little story about the fence panels shaped into the letter H, which suddenly reminded Scott, perhaps still in the fag end of his trip, of Eeyore and his sticks in the shape of an A, except Eeyore at his worst was still more likeable than the owner of the smug and eminently punchable face before him.

"Come on then, Scott" said Maurice, in a sudden surge of bonhomie. "Let's watch the landing. Might be the last chance you get to use that backstage pass"

The arrival of Armstrong and Aldrin on the moon was certainly epochal, but that happened on television, in grainy black and white, whereas the Who were coming in full colour, up close and personal, and their arrival would be followed by something a lot more exciting than a few slow-motion bounces.

No-one anticipated that impending appearance more keenly than Maurice. More than once he checked the integrity of the plywood H, conferring with none other than Bill Foulk, long-haired sibling of Ron and Ray and according to Maurice the one guy who really knew his stuff about the progressive music scene, not that he seemed that keen to impart much knowledge to Maurice. There was a palpable anxiety amongst the waiting throng, such had been the brinksmanship exercised by Kit Lambert, the Who's whizz-kid manager, so that the moment a flying speck appeared on the horizon was one of high drama, a drama intensified as the red copter came close enough for the words TRACK RECORDS to be read on its side. Here was an image to daunt the afficianandos of the folk movement: an alternative new world of blatant self-aggrandisement, the aggressive, tech-savvy, whirling force of the go-it-alone independent label come to blast the stuffed shirts out of the record business. Down it squatted, like a capitalist arse onto the face of the festival, its downwind fearsome, till the plywood H began to shake, then suddenly disintegrate, fence panels flying upwards like blown litter. Maurice's face turned ashen as wood smashed into the rotor blade, staggering the copter and threatening to turn the world's loudest band into a flaming fireball. Somehow the pilot got the monster down safely, but it was a scowling Daltrey who climbed out amongst the circle of onlookers, followed by an equally glowering Moon, Townshend and Entwistle.

Maurice Moss silently slid his autograph book back into his pocket.

"Good one, Maurice" said Scott.

"Shut up, Rayner" hissed Maurice. The downforce of the helicopter had swept his hair back into an impromptu short-and-sides, and suddenly he was once more that short-trousered firstie with his hands jammed into his pockets to protect his crotch from that ancient tradition known as knackering.

Scott no longer practised those straight-fingered jabs, but he was ready with the verbal equivalent. "Gonna ask Bill if he wants to watch the band with us?" he quipped.

"Fuck off" growled Maurice.

"He might let you join their business" continued Scott. "Aren't they called Fiery Creations?"

Maurice Moss was not amused. "Don't you fucking tell anyone about this" he warned Scott, marching from the scene without so much as a nod to his many friends in positions of influence.

Whatever his misgivings about the Who, Scott was not going to miss them while he still had the VIP pass in his pocket. Hardly had he settled onto his chair, however, when a bizarre sight met his eyes. Swaggering past security was Gerry, dressed in a white sheepskin coat, bandana and copious beads, an attentive girl on either arm. Even at this distance Scott could tell Gerry was pretending to be

Spanish, one of his preferred party pieces, though what else he was pretending to be God only knew.

Scott shrank into his seat, craving invisibility. Having parked his harem, however, Gerry's eyes were everywhere, celebrity hunting, and it was only a matter of time before they fell on Scott. Instantly a look of delight came over him, and his arrival was not long in following. "Scotty!" he cried, lightly clapping Scott's cheeks. "Cheer up, may never happen! Oh, I see it has happened"

"I'm fine thanks" said Scott.

"You look it" replied Gerry.

"I am fine" Scott repeated.

Gerry responded with a line of *Only The Lonely*.

"I've been with people all day" protested Scott.

"Jane Fonda's over there" announced Gerry. "Do you think she'll do a strip, like in *Barbarella*?"

Scott studied Gerry's eyes. Was he on speed, or just so high on himself he didn't realise what a tit he sounded?

"You could see her nipples in that scene" said Gerry.

"There's nipples all over this field" noted Scott.

"Not Jane Fonda's" replied Gerry.

"Have you got anything important to tell me?" asked Scott.

"Just reminding you what you said" replied Gerry. "'You have your festival, I'll have mine, and we'll see how we get on'"

Scott had not forgotten what he'd said. Frustration burned within him. People like Gerry should not be rewarded for their cynicism, but clearly they were, even here. Smug and animated, Gerry returned to his seat and laced an arm around each companion. The poor dupes were clearly besides themselves with glee at such suave company, even more so as the famous four took the stage, Daltrey a whirlwind of fringes, Townshend like a Bond villain's lackey in his white boilersuit. Scott's anticipation was equally keen, but that soon turned to shock and awe as the Who launched into their first number at a volume which would have woken the dead in Wootton churchyard. John Thunderfingers Entwistle took lead vocal, fingers as fast and powerful as piano hammers, while Scott jammed his own fingers into both ears to alleviate the pain.

Woodstock had clearly transported the Who onto a high of self-belief. As the crowd lapped up their high-intensity rock and roll, it became awfully apparent to Scott that Gerry had been right about one thing: first and foremost this was a rock festival, where people had come to get excited by rock music, and the band on stage were masters of that art. When the Who played the blues they made sluggards out of Edgar Broughton, yet they could also throw in killer pop singles and groundbreaking new songs, played in an equally groundbreaking style: not only did they have lead guitar and vocals, but lead bass and drums to boot. And when that famous bass kablammed into the intro of *Pinball Wizard*, a buzz came right up through Scott's scrotum and he was gone. Euphoria suffused him and as always led to sublime fantasies of what he might himself achieve, maybe that very night at the bonfire jam, maybe up on that stage the year after next. What was Tim doing these days? The chemistry between Scott and Tim was electric, easily the equal of Mick and Keith, John and Paul. Yes, that was it, Scott and Tim would get together with the superstar remnants of another local band, the Purple Ends, maybe, and they'd be just like Frampton, Marriott and co in Humble Pie after the disintegration of the the Small

Faces and the Herd. People even said Scott looked a bit like Peter Frampton, a bit effeminate with curly hair and kissy lips, a comparison which didn't bother him in the slightest.

Africa. That was the place for them to make it. They'd be taking the music back to its roots, but no-one would have heard anything like it, and soon Scott would have hundreds of people hanging round him, natural, native people, just like that band at the Island Industries Fair. Scott would wear a white cotton shirt with no collar, a thin veneer of sweat over his brow, playing his songs in the marketplaces and the midnight cafes, inspiring his audience to stand up for their rights...

The vision was fading. The tempo had slowed. Angelic harmonies were breaking out. *Tommy Can You Hear Me?* echoed round the arena, not entirely unlike a show tune.

Actually, Scott had never been that keen on *Tommy*, not the whole concept thing, anyway. It seemed very contrived. And once you got past those great pieces of rock...yes, a bit like a West End show. And what could be more deadly than that? Rock music should have nothing to do with the West End.

Peter Brook's dissection of theatre, *The Empty Space*, had been a big influence on Scott. He brimmed with indignation at the thought of the Deadly Theatre and buzzed with appreciation of the possibilities of the rough type. At the suggestion of the head of English he had digested the book while rehearsing the role of De Candia in the Royal Hunt of the Sun, a school play chosen by the English Department not only for its fulsomely anti-imperialist message but also for its occasional, but not excessive use of swearwords. Jim Potter and his colleagues enjoyed putting the head on the spot, testing his boundaries just as keenly as might a rebel pupil. Scott was positively encouraged to project the word 'shithouse', ensuring this reached that imaginary hard-of-hearing parent in the middle of the back row, in which case it would surely not be missed by the man in the mortar board in the middle of the front one.

Deadly Theatre, on the other hand, had one defining characteristic: it failed to challenge. It gave the audience exactly what they were expecting. No-one would have called *My Generation* deadly when it first burst onto the airwaves, but as the Who began their customary trashing of equipment, Scott couldn't help but wonder how long the famous four would carry on performing this well-rehearsed rite. If Moon's exploding drumkit or Townshend's bouncing guitar ever damaged Daltrey's hair that would surely be the end of it.

Scott's cynicism, however, was neither here nor there. Just as at Woodstock, the Who's set had been a triumph. Gerry hugged his companions in unalloyed delight, the crowd bayed for more, and backstage Fat Mattress no doubt cursed the order of play. Soon the queues for the toilets would be outnumbering the audience and the catharsis would be complete.

EIGHT

Sleep was very much an optional extra at the second Isle of Wight Festival of Music, particularly for those, like Jayne and Dave, billeted in the disco tent, where the revelling went on into the early hours, but also for those who either could not come down from the evening's live fare or were too full of anticipation of the messiah's imminent arrival. This ensured there was no shortage of bodies to build Toby and Clem's bonfire, nor to bring their drums, guitars, harmonicas, life stories and astrology charts. The memory of the Moody Blues provided a common currency while the coldness of the wind pushed strangers together like moonlit cattle. As the inhabitants of Wootton Bridge switched off their tellies and downed their cocoa, thankful that the racket was finally over, the spectre of communal living was rising, seemingly unstoppable, in the nearby fields.

Scott, for now, was committed to that cause, since a good performance at the jam would surely draw Jayne back towards him, wiping out the memory of his intemperate diatribe against Dave. Arms full of snaffled twigs and branches, he played a key role in the inevitable cabal of men bringing fire to the tribe, while offering hellos to the ragbag assortment of refugees drawn to their corner of the camping field.

Scott's family had not yet graduated to central heating and he was well versed in the art of firemaking:

the balls of paper at the base, the criss-cross of thin tinder, yesterday's half-burnt coals, or in the case of the outdoor bonfire, the driest branches at hand. His expertise soon impressed the Alleynians, and as the fire crackled into life all three stood hypnotised by its prehistoric magic, talking easily. Yes, *Nights in White Satin* was unquestionably the highlight of the evening. No, it wasn't mawkish exactly, just sad and wistful and aching with love. Yes, Justin Hayward was very charismatic, and if you were homosexual, which neither Toby, Clem nor Scott were, you might well find him irresistible.

"Nice fire".

Joe had approached from his bunker, well-prepared for the weather in his sheepskin and knee-high boots.

"We're going to toast some crumpets when the flames die down" announced Scott.

"Crumpets?" repeated Joe.

"Yeah, crumpets" replied Scott, who had taken a few tokes on Clem's joint and was not fully up to speed with the Atlantic cultural divide.

"Are they something you have with Marmite?" enquired Joe.

"Yes, I've got some Marmite actually" enthused Scott.

"I'd like to try that" replied Joe.

Scott brimmed with satisfaction, proud again to be English, land of crumpets, Marmite and the Moody Blues. "Did you have bonfires at Woodstock?" he asked.

"Hell no" replied Joe. "Too much rain"

"It's not raining here" observed Scott, fatuously, as if lack of rain was a general characteristic of the British Isles.

"No, we've been kinda lucky" replied Joe. "Let's hope it holds off for Dylan"

"I thought Dylan had the power to stop it" quipped Scott, immediately realising what a stupid thing he had said, product of the night's euphoria and THC.

Joe, nevertheless, laughed. "Maybe!" he replied, then slapped Scott on the back and ambled off to greet a friend, leaving Scott eager as a puppy to make his next international contact.

He did not have to wait long. Javier had arrived, greeted with a self-consciously continental embrace by Toby. Sporting a floppy hat with a feather, a Davy Crockett jacket and a blousy scarlet shirt, Javier was extrovert to a fault, and his bright eyes and keen white teeth glinted in the firelight. On his back was a guitar and in his sights was Scott, introduced by Toby as a fellow musician. "We jam together?" he asked.

"I suppose so" replied Scott.

Javier swung the guitar from his back and held it out towards Scott, indicating with a nod and eager grin that it was his for the taking.

"In a bit maybe" said Scott.

Javier offered the guitar a little closer, his nods and grins becoming more urgent.

Scott took the guitar.

"Play something" said Javier.

Scott's inhibitions returned with a vengeance. He was a competent though limited guitarist, but his aim had been to meld with the other instrumentalists once the night was worn down, not produce a solo party piece from cold.

Scott laboriously strummed the chords to *In The Year 2525,* keeping his eyes firmly fixed on the fretboard. He did not need sight, however, to sense the attention focussing on him, driving all confidence from his fingers and all alternatives from his mind. *In the Year 2525* was built on the repetition of four descending chords, and the more self-conscious Scott became, the more unable he was to break free from that musical prison.

Suddenly Scott's turgid strumming was interrupted a short complementary trill. Javier had found a second guitar and was initiating a conversation in the universal language of music, his eyes fixed on Scott's with unnerving resolution. Scott flashed a nervous smile and ploughed on with his descending chords, while Javier inserted merry little bursts, clearly intended to energise the situation.

The soft patter of bongos broke out. Scott felt duty bound to give his chords a little more emphasis, to which Javier responded by yet more animated replies. There were a couple of whoops from the assembled group, at which Scott began to attempt some choppy staccato, greeted with eager nods of approval from Javier and a burst of lead guitar.

At this point a paralysing thought struck Scott. This jamming business, this escalating call and response, was exactly like making love, or at least the kind of heavy petting he had enjoyed with Maxine Ashe. He had been entirely alone with Maxine, however, not watched, egged on and applauded by a crowd of strangers. Ackermann's wanking club paled by comparison.

Scott's eyes refixed themselves onto the fretboard. It was imperative he did not respond to Javier's courtship in any way. The chords had to be played guardsman straight.

Frustrated by this sudden loss of empathy, Javier hammered out increasingly desperate phrases, while attempting to bring his face into Scott's sightline, no matter what contortion this involved. Scott's response to this was to play the chords with even less enthusiasm and virtually no volume.

Javier, eminently sensitive to his musical partner's moods, softened his own contributions to fluttery arpeggios.

Scott played even quieter. Javier's licks became as gentle as the sea caressing the shore.

Hell, thought Scott. This is even more like making love.

At which point Jayne appeared.

Had he not chanced an upward glance, Scott might have missed the opportunity he had craved all evening. But there she was, arms folded, perusing the jam session with an amiable objectivity. The warmth of the now raging bonfire was nothing to the warmth that Scott now felt within, as if a thousand Justin Haywards were belting out that yearning chorus over a PA the size of France.

Scott stepped up his strumming.

A delighted Javier accepted the challenge.

Scott threw in a couple of fast right-hand flourishes.

Javier executed an excited trill.

Scott began to drive, harder and harder.

Javier's fingers became no more than a blur.

Suddenly it was open season. Half the assembled company piled in, making use of any instrument they could find. The jam moved inexorably towards a frenetic climax, or rather, series of climaxes as there was no bandleader to indicate the end was nigh. This, surely, was deeper music from before the dawn of time, elemental, and when it finally ended Scott the atheist was firmly convinced he had shamanic powers. His eyes hungrily sought Jayne's approval.

"Very good" she said, applauding lightly.

"The action was a bit high on that guitar" commented Scott.

"Mm" replied Jayne. "I don't know what it means, but it sounds good"

There was a brief silence.

"So" said Scott, anxious to make hay, "we meet again"

"I'm a sucker for punishment" replied Jayne.

"I doubt that" said Scott.

Jayne gave a wry smile, then pulled out a tobacco tin. "Fancy a joint?" she asked.

"Ok" said Scott.

Jayne got to work with typical diligence and practised dexterity, attaching two rizlas end to end by means of the residue of a third one's gum, then heating a lump of paki black over a matchflame till it was soft enough to sprinkle over a bed of tobacco. A piece of card from the rizla packet served as a roach, then the whole thing was rolled, licked, and coaxed into perfect shape for a smoke. Jayne's know-how mesmerised Scott, who seized the proffered joint eagerly once Jayne had taken her own luxuriant drags, secretly relishing the sharing of her saliva.

The dope was strong. Scott's restless brain sank into a warm herbal bath, melting away the aches and pains of the day.

"You pull some funny faces when you play guitar" commented Jayne.

"Do I?" said Scott.

"You shouldn't frown so much" asserted Jayne.

"It's my natural look" replied Scott.

"You look better when you smile" said Jayne.

"So do you" replied Scott.

Jayne responded with a horribly false grimace.

"Not that one though" said Scott.

"Are you going to pass that joint on?" asked Jayne.

Scott, who by now was not even aware he had a joint in his hand, offered it back to Jayne.

"Not to me" said Jayne.

Scott turned to find Wendy next to him, eagerly anticipating her toke. His heart sank a little as the joint then carried on down a long line of ready punters, clearly never to return. That was clearly the protocol, eminently communal, eminently egalitarian, frustratingly inconvenient.

Jayne, on the other hand, seemed quite at ease with the situation, and once dope began to arrive from every direction, Scott warmed to the custom, even if some of the joints were unpleasantly soggy from communal spit. At least none of that spit belonged to Dave, who was conspicuous by his absence, a fact Scott preferred not to question lest Jayne suddenly remember her missing dependent.

Alas, Dave had merely been detained by a previous arrangement, and his arrival, in the company of a tall, big-faced lad had Jayne leaping to her feet.

"Gerard!" she cried.

Jayne threw her arms around the big-faced lad, whose grin was a match for hers. He had the look of a butcher's boy, keen and meaty, with lank hair plastered across his head like pitch.

"How the fuck did you get here?" asked Jayne.

"Magic" replied Gerard.

"Are they still running ferries?" asked Jayne.

Gerard nodded. "Ah, man" he said. "It's heaving over there. Hippies everywhere"

"Did you have a long wait?" asked Jayne.

"I didn't have *any* wait" replied Gerard, a humourous glint in his eye.

"Come on, Ged" said Jayne, with anticipatory delight. "What's the story?"

Gerard paused for a moment for dramatic effect, then eagerly unburdened himself of his secret. "Went to this bar" he recounted, "started talking to this guy, turns out he's a King Crimson freak. So we get talking, I tell him I'm going to the festival, and he offers me a lift...in a fucking speedboat!"

"Oh, never!" exclaimed Jayne.

"And the funny thing is" continued Gerard, "he is actually on speed!"

"No!"

"God's truth. So I'm bombing over the Solent in a fucking speedboat driven by a total fucking speed freak singing *21st Century Schizoid Man* at the top of his fucking voice! Man, I was fucking shitting myself!"

"Oh, that sounds amazing" commented Jayne.

"What, me shitting myself?" asked Gerard.

"I've seen you shit yourself, remember?" replied Jayne, with a grin from ear to ear.

"You wouldn't believe the queues for those ferries" said Gerard. "This place is going to be fucking teeming tomorrow. How many were at Woodstock? It's going to be bigger than Woodstock"

Scott seized his opportunity to intervene. "Joe was at Woodstock" he commented, indicating his American buddy.

Jayne perused Joe with interest, long enough to unsettle Scott. "Oh, this is Scott" she informed Gerard. "Gerard lives with us" she informed Scott.

Gerard nodded a greeting, friendly but with no particular curiosity. He was an odd fish, evidently on the very fringe of society, yet short-haired, wearing tapered jeans and what appeared to be an old school mac. Clearly, however, he had come to party, and it wasn't long before he was summoning up the spirit of his ancestors by means of a fist-shaking, foot-stamping dance. Dave did his best to reciprocate, though woefully out of time, and it wasn't long before the many and varied festival dances were being practised in all their glory: the hammering of invisible drums, the weaving of mystic webs, the series of minor electric shocks. Meanwhile Javier was soliciting Scott for another performance, a song this time, but even with the help of cannabis that was a big step up from strumming along. So Scott sat on the sidelines, hoping to find another way to reawaken Jayne's interest, while the impromptu band launched into a slow twelve-bar blues. This provided the cue for Gerard to make a theatrical grab for Dave and draw him into an intimate and sinuous dance.

Scott was riveted to the spectacle. Was this some bizarre custom of squat-life, to squeeze your friend as if it was the last dance at the Top Rank? Was irony involved? Were they trying to prove how radical they were? Or simply to unsettle the likes of him, in which case they were being alarmingly successful?

The slow dance, however, proved merely to be the hors d'oeuvres. Fully aware that he had the whole crowd's attention, Gerard lowered his mouth onto Dave's and initiated a full-on tongue sandwich, the ferocity of which matched any carnivore's enthusiasm for its prey.

Once the shock had died down, Scott was euphoric. Bumchums! Homos! Suddenly everything made sense – the love and loyalty between Jayne and Dave was exactly like the bond between best girl friends, and Jayne's unwillingness to talk about their relationship was typical of the kind of omerta such marriages involved. Obviously Dave would have needed a lot of protecting from the likes of the Fawley skinheads: a hippie, a teahead, a queer, and unable or unwilling to lift a finger in self-defence.

Suddenly Scott also felt protective of Dave. Yes, he was as nice a guy as you could meet, and who could doubt that beneath the gloopy exterior lurked a truly original and brilliant mind? Dave represented everything the mainstream media deplored, and what did that say for the kind of society they lived in? Scott hated that society, hated it with a vengeance, and any enemy of Straightsville was a friend of his.

"Hey, Scott!" implored Javier, "You'll give us a song now?"

"Ok" replied Scott.

Scott took Javier's guitar with a new resolution. Now the time was finally right to relay to the world what he had practised so often in the secrecy of the garden shed. No song in history, not even *Whiter Shade of Pale* was more haunting than *Something In The Air*, yet the whole thing was a two chord bash, even if the F#m7 stretched

Scott's frustratingly short fingers. How many times had he sung those portentous lyrics in a barely-audible croak, eyes squeezed tight with emotion and tears brimming? Ok, his pitch was far from perfect, but nor was Thunderclap Newman's honky-tonk piano, and that only added to the charm of the song.

Scott executed a quick panorama. Shiny happy people, all getting along, all part of the party, with even the non-musicians clutching a drum or maraca. Toby and Clem, public school renegades, toasting the crumpets on the fire. A field of tents, the vanguard of a new Albion, hemmed in by a creek once peopled by the Romans. The perimeter fence: Dylan's waiting arena.

It was as if all Scott's life had been leading up to this moment.

"Call out the instigators
Because there's something in the air"

Scott's voice was weak, lacking confidence, but was greeted with respect. He pressed on, and as he reached the line *"because the revolution's here"*, the entire assembled company belted out the words in unison, sending a shiver down Scott's spine and uplifting his performance to another level. Yes, now he would show that emotion, the emotion driven down by a thousand school assemblies, that blessed hope whereof he knew and the head was unaware. And yes, he would even attempt that tricky modulation up to F# and G#m7, a sure crowd-pleaser, even if it tore the sinews of his wrists to do it.

Thus far Scott had avoided eye contact with Jayne, but with his confidence high he turned his attention directly towards her, giving her an enormous smile, which she greeted with an enthusiastic thumbs-up. It was a magical moment, the icing on the cake, and when Scott climaxed to a great round of applause, reward seemed sure to follow.

Hardly had Scott laid down the guitar, however, when he found himself assailed from an unexpected quarter. "Have you playing the guitar long?" a voice asked. Wendy had stationed herself next to him.

"About three years" replied Scott, anxiously checking Jayne.

"Only three years?" said Wendy. "You're very talented"

"I'm a bit of a jack of all trades, really" replied Scott, cursing his luck as Jayne stood up and moved away from the circle.

"I wish I had a talent for music" sighed Wendy.

"You should just get a guitar and practice" replied Scott, on nurture autopilot.

"No, I've tried" said Wendy. "It isn't for me. But you seem so - "

"Where's Claus?" asked Scott.

Wendy's face hardened. "Gone" she declared.

"Oh?" replied Scott, disguising his relief. "Why's that?"

"Don't ask" said Wendy.

Scott's eyes scanned desperately. He'd lost Jayne.

"What are you doing after the event?" asked Wendy.

"Er...going home, I suppose" replied Scott.

"You know the TUC are meeting on Monday?" asked Wendy.

"No, I didn't" replied Scott.

"Right over there" said Wendy, indicating Portsmouth.

Suddenly Scott's eyes found Jayne. She was sitting in the dugout, talking amiably with Joe.

"If the conference ratifies the sell-out, it's going to affect all of us" declared Wendy.

Scott's irritation with Wendy now bordered on anger. Why had she come and sat next to him, uninvited, what made her think she had the right?

"Actually, I've got to speak to someone" he announced.

"Oh, sorry" said Wendy, unexpectedly. "I know I shouldn't be hectoring you, but I dropped some acid a while ago - I think it's beginning to kick in"

"No matter" replied Scott.

"Oh, but it does matter" said Wendy. "I never know how these things will affect me, and in the past I have spoiled a few parties"

Oh great, thought Scott.

"Have you ever taken acid?" asked Wendy.

Scott did not even hear the question. To his astonishment and horror, Jayne and Joe were snogging.

"Have you ever taken acid?" Wendy repeated.

Scott turned on her. "In my opinion" he declared, "people who think Russia is paradise are mentally ill"

Wendy's jaw dropped. She was used to being insulted, particularly with Russia jibes, but never so randomly. Scott, however, was on a mission. Without excuse he abandoned Wendy, seized a crumpet from the plate being prepared by Toby, and marched over to Joe's dugout.

"I've got a crumpet" announced Scott, proffering the said item.

"Sorry?" replied Joe.

"You wanted to try a crumpet" Scott reminded him.

Joe laughed softly. "Come on, man" he said. "Not now"

"I'll put it by for you" declared Scott.

"Thanks, man" replied Joe.

"I couldn't find the Marmite" added Scott.

"Ok, man" replied Joe. "That's cool"

Joe attempted to refocus on Jayne, but she by now was staring fixedly at Scott with a bruised intensity. As Scott retreated towards the fire, she pursued him.

"Oy!" she called.

Scott turned. He was quite afraid.

"What was that about?" demanded Jayne.

"He said he wanted to try a crumpet" explained Scott, lamely.

"That was extremely rude" declared Jayne.

"So was snogging him" replied Scott.

Jayne was furious. "What's that got to do with you?" she demanded.

Scott improvised feverishly. "It's a jam" he declared. "It's everyone doing stuff togther as a group. Not going off on their own and snogging people"

"Sorry" said Jayne, sarcastically. "I didn't realise there was a book of rules. Have you got a copy?"

"Just cos he's an *American*" sneered Scott.

Jayne gazed in disbelief. "Scott, you sound about ten years old" she declared.

"It's true!" continued Scott. "It's just like in the war, when they had nylons and lipstick"

Jayne spluttered into laughter.

"Don't laugh at me!" cried Scott. High and tired, he was verging on hysteria. There were anxious glances from the other partygoers.

"What's the matter?" teased Jayne. "Did you want a kiss?"

Scott's tantrum was stopped in its tracks.

"I'll give you a kiss" continued Jayne. "Do you want a kiss?"

"Yes" peeped Scott.

Jayne seized the back of Scott's neck and drew his mouth down onto hers. Scott's head swam at the depth and succulence of their sudden intimacy; Jayne kissed for real. Was her snog with Joe that intense? Of course not. There was enough chemistry between Jayne and Scott to fertilise the island.

"See?" she said, releasing him. "Plenty to go round"

Yes, thought Scott, and then we'll get a lovely cottage for two in a sea of delphiniums.

"Hey!" called a new voice. "Can anyone join in?"

Inevitably it was Javier. But Scott's displeasure was tempered by the fact that Javier had his arm around a new arrival, plump, vivacious and kissy-lipped. Both of them showed a full set of white teeth the bite of which would surely be fatal, but biting was evidently not what they had in mind. Before any discussion could be had, the four were locked in a standing scrum, Scott facing the inviting features of the woman he had never seen before. A brief dramatic countdown from Javier, and the game was on. A kiss for the kissy woman, a kiss for Jayne, the offer of a kiss from Javier, then laughter, a deep breath from all, seconds away, round two.

It wasn't long before the scrum had grown, like a cell dividing and subdividing to create a new life form, a form entirely devoted to the pleasure of kissing. Vaguely Scott wondered if those Reichian communes were like this, in which case telly would surely be redundant, in which case the advertisers would go bust and a new society would be imminent. Then Jayne's mouth would arrive again and he would remember the lovely cottage for two, where a glass of wine in front of the telly would be paradise.

And then, into the midst of the feast, came Banquo's ghost. No-one else seemed aware of Gerry's arrival, but the spectre of his former friend brought a sudden and profound chill to Scott. Gerry's scowl suggested Scott had done him some terrible injury, but when Scott departed the scrum to attend to the matter, it was no surprise that Gerry's concerns were purely selfish.

"Have you seen my toggies?" he asked.

Scott looked blank.

"Toggies!" repeated Gerry. "Rubbers!"

"Oh" replied Scott. "Weren't they in with the sardines?"

"They're not there now" replied Gerry.

"I haven't had them" said Scott.

"I never thought *you'd* had em, Scott" scoffed Gerry.

The kind of conversation which was common currency at Isaac Watts now seemed to belong to another planet. Scott felt no need to reply: his presence at the heart of the party had said it all.

"*Scheisse*" moaned Gerry. "How did I find the only girl here who isn't on the pill?"

"Have you checked all your pockets?" asked Scott.

"They're not in my fucking pockets!" exclaimed Gerry. With an exasperated sigh he disappeared back into the tent, from within which came the sound of more *fucking*s and the flinging of objects. But there was worse to come.

"Scott" demanded Gerry, reemerging, "where's the tape recorder?"

"What?" said Scott. He crawled into the tent to conduct his own investigation. No, not in the corner at the back under the haversack...not in the haversack...not hidden by the sleeping bags...gone.

A feeling as bleak as the moon swept over Scott. "It was there last time I looked" he told Gerry, lamely.

"You better bloody find it" replied Gerry.

"I can't understand it" said Scott.

"Has anyone been in the tent?" demanded Gerry.

Suddenly the events of the afternoon returned to the forefront of Scott's consciousness, and with it the absolute conviction that Cressida had taken the tape recorder. Did anyone else know she had been in the tent?

Right on cue, Toby homed in on the conversation. "Is anything the matter?" he asked.

"Our tape recorder's been stolen" snapped Gerry.

"No!" replied Toby, dismayed.

"Don't know why you're surprised" said Gerry. "It's worth eighteen quid"

"People have even left their stuff in the disco tent" replied Toby. "None of it's been touched"

"Welcome to the real world" replied Gerry.

Toby frowned. "Are you sure you haven't put it somewhere else?" he asked.

Gerry snorted. "Like where?" he replied.

"I don't know" said Toby.

"That's right, you don't" replied Gerry.

"He's only trying to help" intervened Scott.

"Did you let anyone in the tent?" repeated Gerry, returning to his former line of attack.

"Um…" began Scott, glancing at Toby.

"So you have" replied Gerry. "You wouldn't go 'um' if you hadn't"

Scott decided that partial honesty was the best policy. "Cressida did have a lie down for a bit" he admitted.

"Ah, Jesus!" cried Gerry. "And did you keep your eye on her?"

"Not all the time, no" replied Scott.

"Oh, I don't think Cressida would -" began Toby.

"You better find her then, hadn't you?" said Gerry.

"I really don't think -" began Scott.

"You let a nutter in the tent" snapped Gerry, "and the tape recorder goes missing. What, do you think that's just a fucking coincidence?

Toby adopted a pained expression. "I think the normal principle is innocent until proven guilty" he asserted.

"We're not in fucking court" sneered Gerry, "we're at a fucking rock festival"

"I don't think you should call her a nutter" declared Scott.

"Ah, Jesus!" exclaimed Gerry. "What's wrong with you fuckers!? She's just stolen our tape recorder!"

There was a pregnant pause, during which Scott realised just how tired he was and how cold the night had become.

"Well, what you going to do about it?" demanded Gerry.

"We could tell the police" suggested Scott.

"Oh no, don't do that" said Toby.

"Will you stay out of this?" snapped Gerry.

"I'll get it back" said Scott, anxious to put an end to the discussion.

"You better" replied Gerry.

"I will" repeated Scott.

"You better" repeated Gerry.

At this point the conversation did indeed come to an end, but it was not by Scott's doing. A piercing scream from Wendy was followed by frenetic attempts to calm her as she raved in horrible agony. The acid had kicked in and she was seeing Jan Palach's face in the flames.

Only Jayne seemed oblivious to the drama. She had wandered off in the direction of the creek and was now locked in an ardent embrace with Dave.

NINE

Gerard had not overexaggerated. All through the night they came, all next morning as well, tramping up Palmers Road in various states of preparedness, dog-eared, ferry-sick, with or without tickets, determined either way to witness the prophet's second coming. The newspapermen were busy too, wiring photos of litter, foam and nudity, seeking out any resident with a grudge, but playing their part in the Dylan hype as well. With up to a quarter million expected, and incalculable numbers wishing they were there, it was as well for editors to be circumspect.

Not so Mark Woodnutt MP, well aware of his own constituency, filing away the reports of public urination, graveyard desecration, garden trespass, dirt, decadence and drug abuse. To the local Conservative Party and their followers, there was no question the event should never be taking place, and moves were already afoot to ensure its like would never be seen again. Loud music was one thing, revolution entirely another, and as the saying goes, nowhere are the left better organised than in the minds of the right.

Back at base camp, however, all the talk was of the missing tape recorder. The new movement was defined as much by honesty as love – indeed, how could there be love without that honesty? Jayne and Dave had not thought twice about leaving their sleeping bags and meagre possessions in the disco tent, and after the raving masses had departed each night, they would find those bags neatly rolled and put out of the way of the dancing feet. Sure, there were a few rogues selling aspirin as Mandrax, and Gerry with his ill-gotten pass-outs, but wholesale burglary was another matter.

"Is it possible she took it by accident?" asked Toby, over a very late breakfast.

"Oh, come on, Toby" chided Clem.

"No, I mean, she might have borrowed it, and meant to bring it back, then lost her way or something" suggested Toby.

"I think she knows her way here now" replied Clem.

"Maybe she fell asleep" suggested Toby.

No-one was impressed by Toby's line of thought.

"But why?" pleaded Toby. "Why should she want to do a thing like that?"

Scott said nothing. His head was still doped, not enough for pleasant mind-wanderings, but sufficient to fug his thoughts. More than anything he wished the whole tape recorder business would go away and leave him lost in lovesick misery.

"We still don't know it was Cressida" Clem pointed out.

"That's true" agreed Toby, hopefully.

"It could be the miniature dog with the giant-sized anus" quipped Clem. It was not the first time he had returned to this subject.

"You should write about that dog for your magazine, Clem" suggested Toby.

Scott seized the chance to change the subject. "What magazine's this?" he asked.

"It's a satirical review" replied Clem.

"Which no-one understands" added Toby.

"Which Toby doesn't understand" countered Clem.

"What's it about?" asked Scott.

"Anything" replied Clem.

Scott was possessed of a sudden vision, something he was prone to, of never returning to Southampton, joining forces with Clem, and producing a paper to rival *Oz*. "How do you print it?" he asked.

Clem's answer was evasive. He didn't want to admit being dependent on his dad's successful business.

"I used to do a paper" said Scott, eager to impress. "I ran it off on an old duplicator"

"Hmm" said Clem. "Hard work"

"Used to take me all weekend" replied Scott.

"You should join forces" suggested Toby.

"Yeah!" said Scott, grateful it was Toby who'd made the suggestion. "We could do a special on the festival"

"That would be difficult" replied Clem, "unless you move to London"

"Or you move to Southampton" countered Scott.

Clem and Toby exchanged a knowing glance. Scott felt embarrassed. "It's a bigger city than people think" he said, weakly. The fantasy that he could leave everything behind and start this new life was strengthening. Despite his many arguments with Gerry, Scott was not completely sold on a life at university, just a bigger life.

"What's your magazine called?" asked Scott.

"*Insurrectum*" replied Clem.

Scott's heart sank.

"With the *rectum* bit in capitals" added Toby.

Scott's heart sank further.

"It's mainly for school consumption" explained Clem. "But who knows?"

"You might have to change the title" suggested Scott, testing the waters.

"Maybe" replied Clem.

Scott's fantasy was reborn. Move to London...find a squat...free love, group massage...Jayne's squat burnt to the ground, Dave tragically killed...Jayne wandering homeless, sees familiar figure selling Rubber Dog...

"Maybe you should just let it go" suggested Toby, rudely interrupting Scott's flight of fantasy with an unwelcome return to the subject of the Phillips 3302.

Clem gave a sigh. "Is this Castaneda again?" he asked.

"Nekkhamma, actually" replied Toby.

"God help us" said Clem. "Not Buddhism"

Toby shook his head vehemently. "You really are going to have to stop being so dismissive, Clem" he asserted. "It's very arrogant"

"Yes, master" replied Clem.

"Western culture is too obsessed with material goods" commented Toby.

"But Toby" replied Clem, "if Scott hasn't got a tape recorder he can't record Dylan's concert".

"He could record it up here" claimed Toby, tapping his head.

"Oh, come on, Toby" scoffed Clem.

"It is possible" assserted Toby. "If we weren't so dependent on technology, we would develop those kinds of abilities. What about the time when there were no books or records? Amcient people passed everything down by word of mouth"

"Toby" replied Clem, "Scott isn't going to develop the ability to memorise an entire concert in the next nine hours"

Scott had never really had an advocate before, let alone one as eloquent as Clem, and enthusiastically joined the fray. "Isn't Japan Buddhist?" he enquired.

Toby paused for thought. "I think it's Shinto" he replied.

"No, Scott's right" asserted Clem. "Buddhism is the main religion of Japan"

Reassured, Scott moved in for the kill. "So how come Japan is full of material goods?" he asked.

Toby frowned. "They're obviously not following the teachings" he complained.

"No" said Clem. "Because they're capitalist!"

"Well, obviously" replied Toby.

"Everything is secondary to the profit motive" asserted Clem.

"It doesn't have to be" replied Toby.

"If you say so, Toby" said Clem, clearly tiring of the conversation.

"If people refuse to co-operate" continued Toby, undaunted, "then society will have to change. That is the principle of passive resistance"

"Tune in, turn on, drop out" droned Clem.

"Timothy Leary" said Scott, anxious to prove his knowledge of the counterculture, but to his embarrassment failing to get the anticipated red tick from either Clem or Toby.

Clem finished his breakfast and slid his empty plate over Toby's, in the same languid, lazy manner he employed for every task. "So what do you propose to do, Scott?" he enquired, suddenly adopting the rather formal tone of a lecturer expecting an essay.

"I'm still pondering that" said Scott.

"Do you want to come with us?" asked Clem. "We're going to check on Wendy"

"Ok" said Scott.

Clem and Toby exchanged another of those looks which suggested that, despite everything, Scott was still the outsider.

*   *   *   *

Wendy's new place of residence was the St John's Ambulance tent, where she lay across three chairs like a cut-price tableau of Queen Victoria's deathbed. Wendy had come down now, but as she soon explained to her new audience, had not slept a wink and was in a fragile condition.

Toby and Clem engaged quite professionally in amicable chit-chat, mainly about that afternoon's line-up, while Scott remained at a distance. He remembered all too clearly his capricious attack on Wendy, but as he soon discovered, she had either forgiven or forgotten.

"Hello, Scott" she said, establishing eye contact.

"Hi" said Scott.

"You can come closer" said Wendy. "I don't bite"

Clem and Toby made way. Scott advanced to the makeshift bedside, unsure what to expect but feeling he had to do his best.

"Hello, Scott" Wendy repeated.

"Alright?" said Scott.

"Not really" said Wendy.

Scott made no reply.

"They tell me I can have flashbacks at any time" continued Wendy. "That's a frightening thought"

"I had a bad trip yesterday" replied Scott, helpfully.

"It's not just me then" said Wendy, with evident relief. "Everyone else seems to be having such a great time"

"I'm sure they're not all having a great time" replied Scott, reassuringly.

Wendy smiled. "You seem like someone I can talk to" she said.

Scott, who had been about to check his watch, fought the urge. Wendy drew herself up slightly and perused him. "You're very good-looking you know, Scott" she said.

Scott glanced anxiously behind him. Clem and Toby were nowhere to be seen.

"There's nothing wrong with men looking feminine" continued Wendy.

"Thanks" said Scott.

Wendy drew herself up a little further and fixed Scott with steely eyes. "There's a lot of fucking going on at this festival" she observed.

"I'm sure there is" replied Scott, doing his best not to sound shocked.

"You don't mind me talking to you like this, do you?" Wendy enquired.

"No, it's fine" replied Scott.

"It's just that with Claus I felt I had to watch everything I said" Wendy declared.

"No, you can say anything you like to me" replied Scott, suddenly a man of the world, albeit one who might regret it.

"What do you think of me?" asked Wendy.

"You're fine" replied Scott.

"You don't think I'm too intense?" asked Wendy.

"You can be sometimes" replied Scott.

"It's opened me up, this festival, it really has" declared Wendy.

"Good" said Scott.

There was a pause.

"He wanted to recruit you, you know" declared Wendy.

"Yes, I thought so" replied Scott.

"I told him you weren't ready" said Wendy.

"I'm more into like, alternative kinds of things" said Scott.

"Of course" replied Wendy. "You're still at school"

Scott bridled a little. "No, I think that's just the way I am" he declared.

"You won't think like a worker till you are a worker" responded Wendy.

Again Scott bridled. Wendy had clearly mapped out a future for him which was not his intention. "Actually I'm thinking of starting a magazine" he declared.

Wendy sighed. "This is my dilemma, Scott" she said. "I can't carry on with the party any more, but who else has such roots in the workers' movement? I don't want to end up like these anarchists"

"What anarchists?" asked Scott.

Wendy cast a vague hand around herself. "Have you thought about coming to Portsmouth?" she asked.

Scott sought an exit. "I thought you were leaving the party" he replied.

"I could never stop being an activist" responded Wendy. "That would be like death"

"I have to get home" said Scott.

"I'll pay for a hotel room" replied Wendy.

"I don't think so" said Scott.

"And I'll suck you off" continued Wendy.

"Pardon?" said Scott.

"You heard me" said Wendy.

Scott's heart began to thump. There was nothing about Wendy which attracted him, but nor was there anything offensive about her. Her eyes were as cold and grey as those Pompey ships, her lips were thin, but everything was vaguely symmetrical, and did you actually have to fancy someone who gave you oral sex?

"Do you mean now?" he heard himself saying.

"Well I didn't, but, yes, ok" replied Wendy.

Scott's mouth became very dry.

"Not here, though" said Wendy.

Scott's dope-addled brain struggled to find an appropriate response to Wendy's generous offer. Weren't farmers rumoured to wank off their dogs to ensure their loyalty, and might the CPGB employ similar tactics? Was her disillusion with the party merely a ruse? And didn't she realise he was besotted with Jayne, or was this part of her motivation?

Wendy's openness was catching. "I'm kind of obsessed with someone else" Scott announced.

"Jayne?" said Wendy.

Scott nodded.

"Surprise, surprise" said Wendy.

"What does that mean?" asked Scott.

"She's very pretty" remarked Wendy.

"I wouldn't say that" replied Scott.

"I would" said Wendy.

"I think she looks quite unusual" replied Scott.

"No, she's pretty" said Wendy.

"That's not why I like her though" blabbed Scott. "And anyway, you're..." He trailed off. For the sake of equality, he had felt duty bound to claim that Wendy was just as lovely, but immediately realised what a false note he would strike.

"What?" asked Wendy.

"You are" said Scott, flushing red.

"I'm what?" asked Wendy.

"What we were just saying" said Scott.

"Scott, I don't know what you're saying" replied Wendy.

Scott smiled meaninglessly.

"If I were you" said Wendy, "I should give that Jayne a wide berth"

"What do you know about her?" asked Scott.

"Enough" said Wendy.

"Go on, tell me" pressed Scott.

Wendy was saying no more, but Scott could sense her animosity towards Jayne. He hoped it was purely motivated by jealousy.

"Anyway" said Scott. "I've got to get my tape recorder back"

Wendy was baffled.

"It was stolen yesterday" explained Scott.

"Have you told the police?" asked Wendy.

"No" said Scott.

"I should do that" said Wendy.

This was not what Scott had expected from a person who sold the *Morning Star*. Wasn't Wendy in the crowd the day before when everyone jumped up and flashed v-signs at the police chopper overhead?

"Anyway" said Scott, "I've got to get it back"

Wendy looked a little impatient. "Scott, you're just making excuses" she said.

"No, really, I've got to get it" replied Scott.

"Can't you do it after I've sucked you off?" asked Wendy.

Scott gave this important question due consideration. It wasn't so very long since his sap had first risen in a quiet corner of the school pavilion, and he still remembered his watery-legged uselessness in the house hockey match afterwards. On the other hand, D.H.Lawrence had cured his writer's block by losing his virginity, also at the hands of an older woman, so it was just possible his powers of detection could be strengthened, though frankly, it seemed doubtful.

A decision was impossible. Scott decided to play for time by fishing in his pocket for his programme. "Just got to check the running order" he mumbled.

It wasn't that stunning a line-up. Scott couldn't pretend he was bothered by the prospect of missing the Liverpool Scene, Indo-Jazz Fusions, the Third Ear Band, Pentangle or Gary Farr. Everyone had agreed to meet for Tom Paxton, so that was his guarantee of seeing Jayne, but did he really want to stay on for Julie Felix? On the other hand, if he slipped off for his treat during her set, would his erection stand up to *We're All Going to the Zoo Tomorrow*?

Fuck it, what did it matter? Wendy wasn't Jayne. He'd never see her again. There was no way he was going to Portsmouth with her.

"I'll meet you back here when Julie Felix comes on" he proposed.

"I wanted to see her" replied Wendy.

"I can't do it before" asserted Scott. "I've got to get the tape recorder"

"What about after?" suggested Wendy.

"It's Richie Havens" replied Scott.

"Who's Richie Havens?" asked Wendy.

"You haven't heard of Richie Havens?" said Scott, aghast.

"I'm not that much into music" replied Wendy.

"He's a..." Scott searched for the right word, "...coloured guy"

"That doesn't help me much" said Wendy.

"He's really famous" said Scott.

Wendy shrugged. They really had nothing in common. Scott had no idea why she was interested in him.

"I'll be here when Julie Felix comes on" he said.

"Ok" said Wendy.

Scott beat a hasty retreat, desperate to clear his head and get some perspective before events overwhelmed him. But how could he think clearly when there were so many people, so much expectation, such anarchic energy? For a few seconds he toyed with the idea of walking away, maybe finding a library or a church somewhere, maybe going all the way to the ferry terminal and just sailing back up Southampton Water. Then festival DJ Jeff Dexter plattered *Lay Lady Lay* for the umpteenth time, and all Scott's imaginings went on hold.

Lay Lady Lay had been worming its way under Scott's skin all weekend. It wasn't like any Dylan song he'd heard before. There was something so entrancing about it, those slow descending chords on organ and pedal steel, that soft huge voice, that simple lovely melody…with 2000 watts behind it, it really did sound like the voice of God, calm, reassuring, seductive.

Tears welled up in Scott's eyes. He had not cried since he was a child and quickly choked them back. Then he abandoned all immediate plans and walked into the disco tent.

Scott knew roughly where Jayne would be sleeping, but was unprepared for the sheer size of the dormitory, a homeless shelter on an epic scale. There were pockets of weary action and a few empty spaces, but most people were still asleep after the previous night's partying, strewn in various poses beneath blankets, in bags, some without any cover at all. The milky light through the canvas and the smell of the grass provided a perfect setting for Dylan's song, and Scott prayed he would find her before it ended. And yes, there she was, that unmistakable short black mop barely visible above the edge of her sleeping bag, just a small triangle of pale clear brow to be seen as she lay still as death on her side, knees tucked up a little. Scott viewed her with insufferable love, hardly daring to breathe, wishing with every ounce of his spirit that he might one day wake up alongside her. Then he glanced to her right and saw Dave's fully-awake eyes staring back at him.

"Have you seen our tape recorder?" Scott blurted.

Scott did not wait for a reply before fleeing. This, truly, was mortification. To make matters worse, Dave's eyes for once were not misted and pink, but clear and mathematical. Dave was not stupid.

A rage began to build within Scott. Dave seemed hell bent on being wherever he was most inconvenient, right from that first time he'd loomed over Scott's shoulder at the record store. But this last crucifying meeting would never have happened without Cressida's stupid act of theft. How right Clem had been to call her an emotional parasite. That tape recorder was bought through hard work – hours of rehearsal, hours of gigs – and the thought it could just be snatched by someone whose sole contribution to music was hanging round dressing rooms...

Scott joined the queue at the information stand, bristling at the numbers ahead of him with their inconvenient concerns. In his head he was composing a message in which neither honesty nor integrity would play a part. When at last his turn came, he was as focussed as a gunsight.

"I need to get a message out on stage" he declared. "Urgently"

A worn laconic man awaited instruction with stoic expression. The stage messages would soon be taking up more time than the bands.

"This is a message for Cressida in the crochet dress" dictated Scott. "A friend of Bob's has something important for her"

"Can you be more specific?" said the guy. "Rikki's got a lot of messages to read"

"I can't" replied Scott. "It's a birthday present and I don't want to spoil the surprise"

"A birthday present" repeated the man, sighing quietly as he jotted the message. "How will she find you?"

"Meet outside the Palmers Road gate" replied Scott, pointing unnecessarily towards that significant location.

TEN

Scott habitually avoided conflict for the very good reason that he had only ever been a victim of it. Bullies at school soon rooted out those who'd been softened up by brutal fathers and elder brothers, so that life became an endless struggle to avoid becoming prey while giving off a scent that every predator in the jungle could smell. The festival had promised the possibility of a new life without this rigmarole, but as Scott waited for the unheralded Gypsy to finish their tiresomely average set, the anger had faded and the old feelings were returning.

It was scarcely imaginable what Dylan was going through, cooped up on his Bembridge farm, waiting for the spotlight to be thrust back on him after four years in the wilderness. It was bad enough to be in that media glare for anybody, but to be cast as a war leader in a conflict between generations, that was true pressure. Maybe the critics were right, that he'd profited from it then ducked back from the consequences, but everyone had a right to privacy, to spend time bringing up their kids, to live a life without strangers banging on their windows.

At least Dylan had support, a houseful of Beatles, a manager, God knows who else. All Scott had was Clem, whose charisma faded notably once removed from his professorial chair. With his hands in his pockets, his gangly appearance and his habit of selfconsciously prowling on the spot, Clem did not inspire confidence for the upcoming showdown. But at least the wait was an opportunity to talk magazines, once Scott had given a full and frank account of his interview with Wendy, minus the bits about Jayne and oral sex.

"Have you thought about having a strip cartoon on the front page?" suggested Scott. "People will buy it if it looks like a comic"

"There are no limits at all on what can be on the front page" replied Clem, "but I can't draw"

"I could have a go" replied Scott.

"Ok" said Clem. "Do you have a subject?"

"I could do like, one of the local residents coming to the festival" suggested Scott.

"Yes, that has comic potential" agreed Clem. "As I say, there are no limits. Everything is subject for humour"

Scott thought about his current situation. "I'm not sure about that" he replied.

"Oh it is" asserted Clem, decisively.

Scott cast his mind about for something unspeakably awful and settled on the death, three years earlier, of more than a hundred infants under thirty feet of coal waste. "What about Aberfan?" he asked.

Clem shrugged. "Why not?" he replied.

"You don't think it might upset some people?" asked Scott.

"That is the role of humour" replied Clem.

"Why?" asked Scott.

"It's just something society needs" replied Clem. His chin had retreated into his throat and his voice was no more than a gargle. Scott so wanted him to be the oracle that Scott's dad had once appeared to be, but that hope was clearly misbegotten.

A few more pilgrims appeared up the mud road. Half-hearted applause signalled the end of Gypsy's act. Rikki Farr took to the stage, suitably hyped and hatted for the big day. He laid into the hacks for the rubbish they were printing – a sure crowd-pleaser - then began the usual litany of lost purses, missing children and friends looking for friends. As Scott heard his own words relayed, he first cringed, then comforted himself with the thought that the ploy would never work.

Scott was wrong. Not five minutes later, bursting through the arena exit like a pip from an orange, came Cressida, eyes urgently seeking her unknown benefactor. As Scott rehearsed his opening line, however, he realised, to his dismay, that she was not alone. Right behind her, clearly in league, was a wire-haired guy in a heavily badged denim jacket, sleeves ripped out to reveal tattooed arms: unmistakably a greaser, and a veteran at that, maybe as old as thirty.

If alone, Scott would probably have melted into the crowd. But Clem was right behind him, and Scott could not look a coward or a fool in the presence of Clem.

"Hi" he said, stepping directly into Cressida's path.

"Oh, hi" replied Cressida, neither fazed nor interested.

"Hi" Scott repeated, momentarily locking eyes with the greaser.

"I've got to meet someone" replied Cressida.

"It's me" said Scott.

"You're Bob's friend?" asked Cressida.

"Yeah" said Scott.

"You're not Bob's friend" replied Cressida.

By now Scott was on autopilot. "Have you seen our tape recorder?" he asked.

"No" replied Cressida.

"Only it went missing after you'd been in the tent" said Scott.

"I dont know what you're talking about" replied Cressida. As she spoke, her hand went to her shoulder bag, a bag Scott had not seen before, soft, button-covered, and betraying the presence within of something heavy and sharp-edged.

Only now did Scott realise how poorly he'd prepared for the confrontation. He'd assumed that Cressida would simply cave in under pressure, but clearly this was not about to happen, certainly not with the Wild One in tow. Scott could hardly demand that she show him the contents of her bag, or whatever tent in which she was now sleeping, but how else could he expose her thievery?

As it was, it was Cressida who went on the offensive. "I cannot believe you put that message out for me!" she railed. Then she turned to her companion. "I don't even know these guys" she claimed.

At this point Clem elected to intervene. "Oh, come on, Cressida" he said, the posh half of his see-saw accent becoming unfortunately prominent.

"She said she didn't know you, mate" replied the greaser. His voice was not loud, nor particularly aggressive, but there was no mistaking the threat within it.

"How come we know her name?" muttered Scott, without conviction.

"She don't know you, mate" repeated the greaser, and this time Scott got the message. Reason was to play no part in this debate. He and Clem watched without protest as the pair walked away.

"At least we know she stole it" commented Scott.

"That was painfully obvious" agreed Clem.

"We could follow them" suggested Scott.

"What would that achieve?" asked Clem, less than keen.

"She might open her bag" replied Scott.

Neither wanting to be seen to be cowed, Scott and Clem began to shadow Cressida and her companion through the crowd. Rather than re-enter the arena, Cressida made her way round the western perimeter fence which bordered the car parking field. In keeping with the general anarchy of the event, this area had become an overflow campsite, including treehouses and shanty town shacks. Cressida and her friend eventually stopped at one such shack, beside which were three bikes: a Matchless 650, a BSA Starfire, and a Norton Commando. Scott's uncle had successfully indoctrinated him in the superiority of British bikes over poxy Japanese sewing machines, and he instantly judged their riders to be men to be reckoned with. So it proved, as two bigger greasers exited the shack to greet the Wild One, whose gestures indicated he was relaying the story of the two wankers who had disturbed his enjoyment of the festival.

All three lay proprietorial hands on Cressida in the course of this conversation, enough to suggest they did not share Scott's dream of a world beyond private property. Cressida then entered the shack, with which she was clearly familiar, exiting a few minutes later with a bag from which all suspicious bulges had been eliminated.

"She's put it in there" he whispered to Clem.

"What do you propose to do?" asked Clem.

Scott considered. If the greasers continued to act as sentinels, there was surely no way past them, unless, according to an unlikely scenario Scott was beginning to concoct, he befriended them, possibly with the help of Gerry, and turned them against Cressida. As the *Royal George* was in a village, at least half the local lads were greeboes, and Gerry in particular was good at establishing common ground with them. But then he had the advantage of the keys to the *Royal George*'s back bar.

Not all greasers were violent, though many were hardened by conflict with the likes of the Fawley skinheads. Some even laughed when Scott and Gerry imitated their favoured dance, thumbs in belt, shoulders rocking back then heads plunging to either side of their mate's. Though they frequented Gerry's alternative discos, however, they were certainly not hippies, and it was difficult to see the Wild One reacting with a smile to the fact he'd been followed. The situation was just too unpredictable and Scott was not one to take risks where personal safety was involved. Maybe Wendy was right. Maybe the sensible thing would be to report the theft to the police. But that would negate everything Scott had come for, and in any case there were few around and most were in plain clothes busting people for drugs. Clem had explained about the police while Scott was very stoned, something about the state being essentially bodies of armed men protecting the property-owning classes, but it all seemed rather abstract to Scott, who'd grown up in a cul-de-sac with no fewer than five copper neighbours, none of whom were armed, though most of their kids seemed to have unnatural obsessions with weapons.

There was one more alternative. By sheer weight of numbers, Scott and his allies could make the moral argument. This, after all, was Dylan's festival, not a bikers' rally. If Scott could rally just half the people who were at the previous night's party, they could surely confront Cressida and the greasers without violence, especially with dozens of other Dylan fans in close attendance. Such peaceful confrontations, according to Toby, was how all disputes were settled in primitive societies. The fear of being rejected by the tribe was a far more effective motivator than the threat of violence.

Scott outlined this plan to Clem, who greeted it coolly. "I was hoping to hear some music today" he asserted.

"We can get everyone together at Paxton" pronounced Scott, "and it'll be all over by Richie Havens"

"You hope" replied Clem.

"They probably won't even be here" said Scott.

"In which case" replied Clem, "she'll probably take the tape recorder with her"

"I don't think so" said Scott. "She's not going to risk carrying it around now she's seen us. And she's got no idea we've seen where she's put it"

Clem reluctantly agreed to the plan, but his commitment to the cause was looking shaky. He had no more proclivity than Scott for violent confrontation and lacked the burning sense of personal injury.

The new friends parted, Clem to catch the end of Adrian Henri's eccentricities, Scott to seek out a burger and the cover of a certain album, the creators of which were the latest to be rumoured to be appearing with Dylan. Perversely, however, he decided to take the route through the disco tent, where most of the sleepers were now stirring. On the spur of the moment he figured that his earlier indiscretion might be neutralised if he walked straight past Jayne and Dave with his eyes apparently set on some more important goal.

There was one fatal flaw in this plan. Try as he might, Scott could not resist shooting brief glances to his right every few yards, until inevitably he caught a glimpse of Jayne, who just as inevitably caught sight of him. The whole thing happened in a millisecond, but that was enough to cause Scott's stomach to drop and face to flush. He would, nevertheless, have carried on walking had not Jayne called his name.

"Oh – hi" said Scott, with grossly affected nonchalance. Encounter now unavoidable, he began improvising furiously. "I was in here earlier" he gabbled, "only I didn't have my contacts in, and I was trying to see if it was you or not, but -"

"You found it?" interrupted Jayne.

"Yes" replied Scott.

"It's alright, Dave" said Jayne. "Scott's got it"

"Eh?" said Scott.

"Dave's tin" said Jayne.

"What tin?" asked Scott.

"Dave's hash tin" said Jayne.

Scott looked blank.

"You said you found his hash tin" said Jayne.

"I didn't" protested Scott.

"You just said you found it" repeated Jayne.

"No!" replied Scott, suddenly clicking. "I found my contact"

Jayne looked deflated. "Then why were you in here?" she asked.

"Oh, I don't know!" said Scott. "It doesn't matter now". His face was burning with embarrassment and anger. Jayne was acting as if the night before had never happened. Some embarrassment of her own was the least Scott might have expected.

"We'd better go back to the camping field and look for it" announced Jayne.

Scott might have mentioned his own lost property, but why should Jayne be bothered with the trivial matter of an £18 tape recorder when her beloved Dave had lost his dope? Clearly the hapless hippy was helpless without his daily fix. Helpless also without Jayne acting as a substitute mother, because that was exactly the role she performed, apart from the perverse tendency to allow his tongue into her mouth.

Jayne, Dave, Gerard and Scott set off in the direction of the camping field. More by accident than design, Scott fell behind the three housemates, his resentment growing as they shared a packet of biscuits between them. Dave got the last one, then without apparent thought, screwed up the wrapper and dropped it on the ground.

Suddenly Scott's rage resurfaced. All thoughts of his proposed moral alliance were forgotten as he raced up behind the housemates, seized the discarded wrapper and confronted the perpetrator.

"Are you just going to leave this?" he railed.

Dave was stunned silent; likewise Jayne and Gerard.

"Someone else is going to have to pick this up" continued Scott.

"Oh, come on, man" replied Dave, with a little laugh.

"What's funny?" snapped Scott.

"It's just a bit of paper, man" said Gerard.

"Which someone else is going to have to pick up" repeated Scott.

"Listen, man" said Gerard. "You're welcome to your bourgeois values, just don't lay them on us"

Scott's adrenaline, already pumping, switched to full flow. "Bourgeois?" he scoffed. "What's bourgeois about it? The bourgeoisie don't pick up the fucking litter, the workers do". Scott swept a trembling arm around the perimeter fence. "How do you think all this got here?" he railed. "Workers put up the fences, the stage, the shops, the lights…workers like me"

"I thought you were at school" replied Dave.

"How do you think I could afford a ticket?" responded Scott. "I worked for it"

"Well then" said Dave, showing a surprising degree of combativeness. "It'll make more work for someone picking up the litter"

All Scott's simmering fury against Dave rose to the boil. "That's your view of the world, is it?" he snarled. "A place for dropouts to lay about in their own shit while the rest of us clear it up"

"Come on, Dave" said Gerard, coaxing his friend away from the escalating confrontation, only to be pursued by an incandescent Scott.

"You're living in a fucking dream world, thinking this is how you're going to change the world" Scott railed. "The real world's over there, mate!"

Dave and Gerard gazed in bafflement at Scott's pointed finger, which he belatedly realised was directed closer to Osborne House than Portsmouth, something he could not alter without bathetically comic effect. "You probably haven't even heard of the TUC" he mumbled, unconvincingly.

The face that launched a thousand joints had remained remarkably impassive throughout this confrontation, but now Jayne stepped forward to resolve matters. "I'll take the wrapper" she said.

Scott hesitated. He wanted to keep pressing Dave, to push the situation to a crisis in the hope Dave would back down, but at least Jayne offered a resolution without loss of face. And Jayne's eyes, so still in the heat of this conflict, were quite hypnotic to him. He handed her the wrapper.

"I'll catch you up" Jayne said to her housemates. They moved on. "What are you, the litter monitor?" she asked Scott.

Scott seized the opportunity of levity. "Prepositor, actually" he replied.

"Prepositor?" responded Jayne. "What the fuck's a prepositor?"

"Above a monitor" replied Scott.

"Is there a lot of that goes on at your school?" quipped Jayne.

"Ask the head boy" replied Scott.

"Head boy?" said Jayne. "Is that giving or receiving?"

Scott smiled lamely. This was going beyond his understanding, and besides, the sparring was far from playful.

"What's the problem, Scott?" asked Jayne, changing tack.

"Don't know what you mean" replied Scott.

"This whole site's a tip" said Jayne. "Why pick on Dave?"

"It's just the way he did it" replied Scott.

"Have you got a problem with Dave?" pressed Jayne. Scott snorted derisively.

"What does that noise mean?" asked Jayne.

"Why should I have a problem with him?" replied Scott. "He doesn't mean anything to me"

"Well, he means something to me" declared Jayne.

"I gathered that" replied Scott.

"Is that what you have a problem with?" pressed Jayne.

"I just can't stand people who think the world owes

them a living" declared Scott, reverting to one of his father's favourite sayings.

"Yeah, like you know so much about work" replied Jayne.

"I worked for three days to help put this festival on" asserted Scott.

"Big deal" responded Jayne. "I get up at five every morning, five days a week, every week. And just for your information, I'm a cleaner. Only I don't pick up litter. I chase old ladies round a mental ward trying to get the turds off their hands. And in case you're wondering, I fucking hate it. The only thing that's kept me going is the thought of seeing Dylan, so please don't fuck it up for me"

Scott digested the information, momentarily concocting a vague plan by which he would effect the princely rescue of Jayne from her drudgery. "So do *you* think it's alright, dropping litter?" he asked.

Jayne sighed. "It's not like the biggest fucking issue in my life at the moment" she replied.

"But is it right?" pressed Scott.

"Scott, I don't care, do you understand?" railed Jayne. "I just don't want you having a go at my friends"

"Do you snog all your friends?" blurted Scott.

A knowing look came over Jayne. "That's what this is all about, is it?" she asked.

"I just want to know where I stand" replied Scott.

"Right now" quipped Jayne, "in everyone's way"

That was certainly true. Competing herds bustled their way towards the shops, the gates and the camping field, and Scott and Jayne stood at the virtual crossroads. Scott's elucidation would have to wait as the fate of Dave's dope tin once more became the chief concern of the object of Scott's desire.

ELEVEN

If Dylan was the main meal, Tom Paxton was the perfect hors d'oeuvre: a fellow disciple of Woody Guthrie with impeccable protest credentials, Paxton had also penned the lilting *Last Thing on my Mind,* a song occasionally hummed by Scott's mum, the least likely person to protest about anything. Fiery Creations had clearly seen Tom as the man to whet the appetite of bandana-wearing folk without inspiring them to tear down the fences.

According to plan, the Alleynians' growing tribe assembled for Paxton's stint half way back in line with the right hand speaker stack. There was Joe and his American pals, Javier and his international band of gypsies, Jayne and her squatmates, Clem, Toby, two more of their schoolfriends and at least three other faces Scott failed to recognise. Even without those, like Cressida and Claus, who had fallen by the wayside, it was a formidable battalion of alternative-type people. Despite the sullen silence between himself and two of the assembled company, Scott had never had such a feeling of belonging. Nor such a feeling of personal virtue, having abandoned the VIP enclave to be amongst his people.

Gerry would be in that enclave, no doubt. Gerry was no particular fan of Tom Paxton, but in order to pursue his primary aims of making money and shagging women, it would undoubtedly have become necessary to go with the flow and embrace the protest movement. Fortunately Gerry's knowledge of music was sufficiently comprehensive to include the likes of Pete Seeger, Joan Baez and Phil Ochs, and no doubt those very names would right now be escaping his lips to delight the waiting ears of his new harem.

No matter. It was highly unlikely Scott would see Gerry again before returning to the mainland. All that mattered was to victoriously present him with the bootleg tape, to relay the story of the army of moral crusaders, the triumph over the thieving greasers, and the ingenious way the Phillips EL3302 had been smuggled backstage for an exclusive interview which would not only stun the pupils of Isaac Watts, but the citizens of the world.

So ran Scott's thoughts as Tom Paxton began his set and euphoria slowly spread under the dull August skies. Despite the sideburns and moustache he now sported, Paxton still cut a figure any mother would welcome home for tea. But this modest, shiny-eyed man had a burning sense of righteousness which was clearly what the audience had been craving. Just as an acoustic guitar was sufficient for Country Joe to electrify Woodstock, so six strings and a good PA served for Tom Paxton at Woodside Bay. His voice was strong and warm, his humour cutting, his targets well chosen. As the joints circulated round Scott's new tribe, each song was better received than the last.

Buoyed up by the task he would soon face, Scott did not need the weed to heighten his perceptions. Maybe others could function perfectly well under its influence, but he had already established that it was more likely to make him both useless and paranoid in a conflict situation. Not that there would be conflict, in the sense of violent confrontation: if Cressida and the greasers were listening to Tom Paxton as well, would they not recognise Scott as a brother?

Paxton's set ended in a rapturous reception. Encores were a rarity at this festival, but this one could not possibly be denied. The cherubic minstrel returned with *Talking Vietnam Pot Luck Blues*, a song guaranteed to press every button the audience possessed. Jayne's eyes squeezed into crescents of delight. This was the experience that she, and just about everyone else had been saving their money for. One more encore later, and the entire crowd were on their feet, chanting Tom's name with a fervour to rival any cup final.

Circumstances could not be more favourable for Scott. As Paxton made his final, heartfelt farewell and exited the stage, so Scott, heart pounding, called for everyone's attention. He was used to speaking in public, either in school plays or to propose a vote of thanks to his gran for Christmas dinner, but this was of a different order altogether, requiring the crying of havoc and the letting loose of the doves of peace. Pretentiousness was unavoidable.

"As some of you know" he declared, "a tape recorder belonging to Gerry and me has been stolen. I know it's not exactly Vietnam, but for us it's really important. We came here to make a tape of Dylan for all our friends and for posterity because today is a historic day. What has happened is simply wrong and I need your help to right it"

"Wow" said Javier. He was heavily stoned.

"What do you want us to do, Scott?" asked Joe.

"Clem and I think we know who's got it" replied Scott, glancing at Clem for approbation, but getting nothing back. "We think if everyone goes over there together, they might listen to us" Another glance at Clem: still nothing.

"You mean we make a gang?" asked one of Joe's friends.

"Not a gang" replied Scott. "A delegation"

"Heavy" muttered Javier.

There was a silence.

"So who are these guys?" asked Joe.

"Some greasers" replied Scott.

"Greasers?" repeated Joe.

"Bikers" explained Scott.

"Like Hells Angels?" asked Joe.

"Not Hells Angels" affirmed Scott. "And anyway, British Hells Angels aren't like American Hells Angels". It was something he'd learnt from the teenage greeboes at the *Royal George*.

"In what way?" asked Joe.

"They don't carry guns for a start" replied Scott.

"They don't carry weapons?" asked Joe.

"They might carry knives" replied Scott. "I don't know"

"Don't you think you ought to know," suggested Joe, "if you're going to pick a fight with them?"

"I'm not picking a fight with them" protested Scott.

"I'm here for peace, man" asserted Joe, "not to start a war"

"I'm not starting a war!" replied Scott, still hyped from his speech and becoming increasingly irritated.

Joe laid a fatherly hand on Scott's shoulder. "You've got to move on, man" he said.

"In what sense?" asked Scott.

"Rise above it, man" explained Joe.

"How does that help me get my tape recorder back?" asked Scott.

Joe exchanged glances with his pals and smiled gently. "Listen, Scott" he said. "You're a good guy. Why get dragged down to the same level as these assholes?"

"They've got my tape recorder!" protested Scott.

"So what?" replied Joe. "It's just a box of metal and wire"

"See, Scott?" said Toby, seizing his chance to intervene. "Like I said, you've got to let it go"

Scott fumed. "Yeah, well my dad can't afford to buy me one every week" he snapped.

There was a short silence.

"Was that aimed at Toby?" asked Joe.

"Not particularly" lied Scott.

"Seems they've got to you already" commented Joe.

"Yes" barked Scott. "They have got to me, because they've got my tape recorder, and I want it back! What's the point of listening to protest songs and going 'oh, wow, yeah, we've got to stand up for our rights', then you can't lift a finger when someone nicks your things?"

Scott's words were moving nobody. He sensed he was becoming an embarrassment. "My mum gave me money towards that" he said, weakly, and the thought of his mum caused a little break in his voice. She earned eleven pounds a week at the dry cleaners.

"I think people do want to watch the music, Scott" said Clem.

"What, Pentangle or Julie Felix?" scoffed Scott. He had expected at least token suppport from his new friend.

"Hey, don't knock Julie Felix" commented Javier. "Julie Felix is cool"

"Yes, that's why they gave her a TV series" sneered Scott.

"What's wrong with her having a TV series?" asked Toby.

"It proves she's safe" replied Scott, suddenly feeling a camraderie with Gerry, who would certainly share that view.

"She's written some good songs, man" commented one of Joe's friends.

"Yeah, like *We're All Going to the Zoo Tomorrow*" sneered Scott.

"Tom Paxton wrote that song" replied Joe.

Scott looked to Clem like a drowning man. Clem shrugged. "I don't believe that" declared Scott. "Tom Paxton would never write a song celebrating animals being kept in cages" He scanned his audience, many of whom kept their eyes averted, while Gerard and Dave struggled to hold back their amusement. Suddenly the dam burst and a spume of pot-fuelled belly-laughs gushed forth. Scott turned on his heel and, not for the first time that weekend, fought his way towards the exit.

TWELVE

By the time Scott had reached the St John's Ambulance tent, he had convinced himself he was reconnecting with his one true friend at the festival. Maybe Wendy had taken a wrong turn politically, but at least she wasn't all talk. What was more, she didn't pretend to like Scott, she really did fancy him. And while certain people found it necessary to blow hot and cold, to taunt and to tease, she was absolutely straight in her dealings.

Wendy, as it soon transpired, was also reliable. As good as her word, she had remained in the St Johns tent, virtually unchanged since Scott left her, apart from the presence beside her of a young man in heavy NHS specs, one of the many swotty types at the festival who had not yet morphed into true hippies.

Specky four-eyes did not last long. As Scott entered the field, the young man withdrew with commendable humility, leaving the way clear for Scott to resume what he now believed to be the most important relationship of his life.

"Hello, Scott" said Wendy, with a calm, slightly distracted air. "I've had a lovely sleep"

"You missed Tom Paxton" Scott informed her.

"Was he good?" asked Wendy.

"Most people thought so" replied Scott.

"But not you?" asked Wendy.

"I thought his songs a little childish" replied Scott.

"I couldn't comment on that" said Wendy.

"Do you want to go to my tent now?" asked Scott.

"Come on then" replied Wendy.

Wendy gathered her things while Scott, who had thitherto avoided eye contact, took the opportunity to peruse her a little more closely. Her skin was pale and rather unhealthy, her brow high and prematurely lined, marked by high, thin arching eyebrows which might have belonged to Mary Tudor. Her nose was unattractively beaked, and coupled with a prominent chin formed a Daliesque pair of pincers around her thin mouth. Scott had made a wise decision not to allow dope to fire his imagination.

Wendy acted with businesslike singleness of purpose. As they met the burgeoning crowd she took Scott's hand and began to lead the way, presuming an intimacy which was not what Scott wanted at all. A half-hearted attempt at withdrawal proved the tightness of her grip: Scott began to feel like a convict being escorted to trial through a bizarre netherworld, an experience heightened by the eerie and slightly sinister madrigals now issuing from Pentangle on the festival stage.

By the time the pair reached the tent, Scott's half-suppressed doubts had come raging to the surface. He did not know why he was doing this at all. Determined to retake the initiative, he led the way inside and immediately lay on his back, only to find Wendy taking up position alongside him.

"So this is where it all happens" she remarked.

"Does it?" asked Scott.

"Claus told me a few things" Wendy informed him.

"Such as?" asked Scott.

Wendy chuckled knowingly. "I should have warned you" she said, "Claus is a real blabbermouth"

Scott chose not to refute whatever nonsense Claus had been spreading. He did not want to talk about Claus.

"He was never faithful to me, you know" remarked Wendy.

"No?" replied Scott, curtly.

"Every time a new recruit came along I feared the worst" continued Wendy.

"Are we going to…do something?" asked Scott.

"Be patient!" counselled Wendy. She placed a finger on his lips, another presumption of intimacy from which Scott inwardly recoiled.

There was a short silence.

"I wish I could stop thinking about my dad" said Wendy.

Please, no, thought Scott.

"He'll never understand" continued Wendy.

"You're going to tell him?" asked an astonished Scott.

"I'll have to" replied Wendy.

"Why?" pleaded Scott.

"He's been in the party all his life" replied Wendy.

"Eh?" said Scott.

"Dad's a lovely man" continued Wendy, "but too trusting"

"Can we talk about this later?" asked Scott.

"Sorry" said Wendy. "I just know it's going to kill him"

Scott said nothing, hoping, vainly as it happened, the subject would go away.

"Poor guy's crippled with arthritis" continued Wendy. "Lives in constant pain"

"Has he tried paracetamol?" suggested Scott, curtly.

"He's tried everything" replied Wendy. "All that keeps him going is his garden"

Scott checked his watch, only to realise he wasn't wearing one.

"He's made it so lovely, Scott" continued Wendy. "Nothing pretentious, just simple, lovely, homely. Like him" She came up on one elbow and looked Scott in the face. "You remind me of him" she said.

Scott doubted he was one bit like Wendy's father.

"Trouble is, every year it gets harder to dig" continued Wendy. "I dread to think what his life must be like. No relief"

Scott decided to try a joke. "I know what that's like" he said.

"Do you?" replied Wendy. "Why's that?"

They were not connecting at all. The prospect of life in Scott's pants was becoming increasingly remote.

"He liked Claus" continued Wendy. "But then, he never knew about the other girls"

"You should have told him" opined Scott.

"I just thought I had to put up with it" replied Wendy. "But being at this festival has made me see things differently"

"Good" replied Scott, reverting to being an enlightened idealist.

"What's good for the goose..." began Wendy.

"Shouldn't that be 'what's good for the gander'?" quipped Scott.

"You're really good-looking, you know, Scott" replied Wendy. She pulled down his fly.

With sudden and overpowering certainty Scott realised he had made a mistake. This was not going to solve anything. And wait, was it possible to catch VD from oral sex? And what about that playground rumour about the epileptic girl who'd had a seizure while Trevor Benwell's knob was in her mouth? Couldn't LSD trips trigger epilepsy? What if Wendy did suffer a flashback?

Too late. Wendy's mouth was on him. She performed the act with extreme vigour and enthusiasm, or the pretence of it, but it soon became clear that her hard work was entirely in vain. Scott's sacred member was as numb and inert as as the little length of rubber tubing on the end of a bunsen burner.

Unperturbed, Wendy began to make "mm" noises, possibly to inspire Scott, but this only inhibited him further. The last woman to have touched his parts was his mum, a thought Scott summarily banished in a frantic search for inspiration. Pans People wagging the naughty finger...Maxine Ashe's bra...Judy Geeson in *Three Into Two Won't Go...*

Nothing.

Wendy, well used to adversity in her political life, stuck to her task with impressive fortitude. Like a Pompey warship reversing out of port, she manoeuvred her rear in the direction of Scott's face and began wiggling it. Scott first assumed the movement was accidental, then it occurred to him, chillingly, that the nearby arse was intended to stimulate him. Was this, he wondered, a technique which worked on Claus? Did that have something to do with the fact he was German? Scheisse, what else was involved?

Scott put both hands against Wendy's ribs and pushed hard. "Stop" he ordered.

Wendy's face rose up and veered towards Scott, flushed and dismayed. Oh God, he thought. "I'm tired" he said.

Wendy wiped her mouth and dropped back down next to Scott. Overpowered by shame, Scott tucked his sullied willy back into his pants. His mum came to mind. She took the view that the Sixties was a Pandora's box which should never have been opened, and for the first time, Scott wondered if she might be right.

"I think you'd better go" said Scott.

A tense silence ensued.

"Do we still have our deal?" asked Wendy.

"We didn't make a deal" replied Scott.

"I see" responded Wendy.

Another silence.

"I hope you're not telling Claus" said Scott.

"That" replied Wendy, "is the whole object of the exercise"

"Fuck off then" responded Scott.

There was no reply. Scott chanced a quick glance leftwards, only to see the trail of a tear over Wendy's cheek. Sensing more were coming, he crawled out of the tent and lay on one side, head propped, staring fixedly in the direction of the Little Canada holiday camp. The predicted sobs duly ensued: released, choked, released, choked again. Wendy was certainly striving to fight whatever emotions were coming, whereas Scott was struggling to feel any emotion beyond the usual self-pity. Wendy was right, everyone else was having a better time than her, and a better time than Scott for sure.

Pentangle were not finished yet. "Let No Man Steal Your Thyme" rang out over the PA. Scott felt the combined weight of womankind looming threateningly over him, a vast mother against a stupid little boy.

"Scott?" came a call. Jayne was walking towards him, looking concerned.

Scott's embarrassment was complete. "Alright?" he grunted, averting his eyes.

"Who's crying?" asked Jayne.

"Wendy" mumbled Scott.

"What's the matter?" asked Jayne.

Scott shrugged.

"Have you asked her?" asked Jayne.

"She doesn't want to be disturbed" replied Scott. Though his eyes remained on the horizon he could sense Jayne's distrust. Moments later she was at the entrance to the tent.

"Are you alright?" she asked.

The sobbing stopped.

"Wendy?" asked Jayne.

A few more moments elapsed, then Wendy appeared. Her face was red but her eyes dry. "Hello, Jayne" she said, breaking into a grimace of a smile, before walking over to Scott and laying a hand on his shoulder. "Thanks for everything, sweetie" she murmured.

"Bye" muttered Scott.

Wendy left her hand proprietorially on Scott's shoulder, as if it could burn her mark like a branding iron, then sauntered off to become no more than an uncomfortable memory. Scott remained cold, closed and motionless.

"You're flying low" remarked Jayne.

"Eh?" said Scott.

"Your flies are undone" clarified Jayne.

Scott's hand shot to his flies, face flushing as red as the people's flag. Was it possible to hide nothing at this stupid festival? Why, oh why, couldn't Wendy have been better looking?

If Jayne suspected anything, she didn't say. "So what's happening with your tape recorder?" she asked.

"Nothing" mumbled Scott.

"I thought you wanted to get it back" said Jayne..

"I don't want to talk about it" muttered Scott.

"I won't offer to help then" replied Jayne.

Scott said nothing.

"Scott" pressed Jayne, "I'm offering to help"

Scott's eyes remained fixed on the distance.

"You can fuck off then" said Jayne.

"I'm depressed!" snapped Scott.

"You're making me depressed" replied Jayne.

Scott stirred momentarily from his self-pity to turn on his erstwhile friends. "How am I supposed to do anything" he demanded, "when all those fucking hippies want to do is listen to Julie fucking Felix?"

Jayne sniggered.

"What's funny?" snapped Scott.

"Julie Fucking Felix" replied Jayne.

Scott made no reply.

"Sounds like a blue movie" added Jayne.

"I need a fucking gun" asserted Scott, suddenly.

"That's fighting talk, Scott" replied Jayne.

"I mean it!" raged Scott.

"I can get you a gun" replied Jayne.

Now Scott laughed.

"I can get you a gun right now" confirmed Jayne.

"Yeah, right" scoffed Scott.

"My Dad's in the army" replied Jayne.

"You haven't got a gun" said Scott.

"*I* haven't" replied Jayne. "But I know someone who has"

"Who?" asked Scott.

"You try living in a squat" replied Jayne. "You'd soon learn to defend yourself"

"Is it Gerard?" asked Scott.

"It might be" replied Jayne.

"Don't believe it" responded Scott.

"You haven't woken up in the middle of the night with a gang of psycho nutters trying to break your door down" said Jayne.

"Gerard has never got a gun" asserted Scott.

"I never said it was Gerard" replied Jayne.

"Well, Dave certainly hasn't" said Scott, witheringly.

"Do you want a gun?" pressed Jayne.

Scott lifted his eyes. The look in Jayne's was deadly serious.

"If someone here has got a gun" asserted Scott, "you'd better tell me and I'll go straight to security and tell them".

"Scott" replied Jayne, "you're full of shit"

Scott hated her. "Why don't you just fucking leave me alone?" he railed.

"Because I can't stand you being so fucking miserable!" replied Jayne. "I want this to be the best fucking day of my life and I can't enjoy it because I know those fucking assholes have totally fucked you over!"

Scott had not expected this reply, which shocked and pleased him in equal measure. "Do you have to swear so much?" he asked.

"Sorry, vicar" replied Jayne.

"My mum helped pay for that tape recorder" repeated Scott, and again the tide of emotion rose up his throat.

"Yeah, I know, you said" replied Jayne.

"Fucking bastards" muttered Scott.

"We'll get it back" asserted Jayne, with an assurance that filled Scott with foreboding.

THIRTEEN

The island had surely never heard a voice like Richie Havens'. It seemed to rise out of the earth, from the roots and the coal seams, and soar into the heavens, inspiring a kaleidoscopic sunset that filled the sky with florid omens of autumn. The sandalled foot that hammered Woodstock into life now worked its shamanic power on Woodside Bay, so that all that went before seemed no more than the chatter of respectable front rooms. Dylan, it was said, had insisted a place be found for his co-performer from Cafe Wha, and it showed a sublime self-confidence that he did not fear being upstaged.

The huge arena, for so long half full, was now almost packed to capacity, while the VIP area had far exceeded its nominal quota. So too had the disco tent, which the have-nots had turned into a jumble of twisted metal and canvas. Some bright sparks had hit on the idea of climbing onto its roof to get a free view. Others had quickly followed, ignoring warnings from the stage: the collapse of the tent, with appropriate injuries, was grimly predictable.

The only area of the festival more oversubscribed was the greasers' den, in which Cressida had been entertaining throughout the late afternoon. Scott watched the comings and goings with a mixture of disgust and fascination, while Jayne merely hoped Cressida was using adequate protection. At least, she reasoned, the greasers might be weakened by their exertions.

Scott barely raised a smile at this joke of Jayne's. The closer they came to the crux, the more he was possessed by a sense of unreality. The situation he found himself in was so far from any in which he had voluntarily placed himself before. Sure, he had shown bravery to face down his demons and walk out onstage in a packed school hall – but that was merely a play. No-one was likely to hit him, or worse.

There was no going back, however. Jayne's conviction was absolute, and if he was to have any credibility with her, he had to remain beside her. Their mission had granted him exclusive rights to her company, an unexpected, physical luxury: the price of that physical luxury was physical danger.

The end of Richie Havens' set was the signal for Cressida to leave the den and make her way towards the nearest gate. Alongside her was the Wild One; over her shoulder was her button-bag, showing no evidence of a Phillips 3302 within. Frustratingly, however, a gaggle of greasers remained, probably ticketless: alongside the Matchless, BSA and Norton there was now a Triumph and second Norton. Darkness was falling, helicopters circled overhead, and next on stage were the Band, or as some would call them, Bob Dylan's Band.

A couple of greasers wandered dangerously close to the hippie dormobile behind which Jayne and Scott made their reconnaissance. They decided to make themselves scarce for the time being. But with rumours that Dylan was already backstage, they could not afford to wait long.

As they queued for the food tent, Croker's fluorescents flickered then blazed the length of the perimeter fence. The sea of electrons was alive again.

Desperate for distraction, Scott composed lyrics in his head, something about an electric city mocking the sun. As usual they came out like poetry from a grammar school arts magazine, no relevance to his present feelings, no comfort at all.

"Do you want chips, Scott?" asked Jayne. She had reached the counter.

"Can I have a burger?" asked Scott.

"Not if I'm buying it" replied Jayne.

"Forget it then" said Scott.

Jayne purchased her chips, munched a few mouthfuls, then threw the remainder and their Daily Sketch wrapper into the nearest bin. Jayne was evidently more nervous than she let on.

Returning to their vantage point, Scott and Jayne were surprised to find everything quiet on the western front. The den, as far as they could see, was abandoned. There was, however, the possibility that a body, or bodies, lurked within.

Jayne insisted there should be no hesitation. They should check out the den, and if it proved to be empty, conduct a lightning smash-and-grab.

The possibility of a bloodless coup inspired Scott to action. One quick panorama, then he approached the ramshackle structure they had watched so long. Close up, its ingenuity became apparent: a melange of abandoned barn doors, broken gates, parts of farm machinery, even turf: nothing better summed up the spontaneous side of the festival, driven by need, not profit, people, not promoters. Toby would undoubtedly have seen something ideal in it.

Scott peered through the makeshift door. The den was empty. Hastily he wrenched the door aside, eyes scanning the chaos within: two sleeping bags laid out on the floor; a petrol can; torn papers, rags, a filthy cushion, an empty Party Seven, discarded food wrappers, and in the corner an assortment of plastic bags. The smell was rank, but this was no time for prudery: those bags had to be searched.

Hardly had Scott laid a hand on the first bag, however, when there was a yell:

"Get the fuck out of there!"

"Get out, Scott!" cried Jayne.

Scott leapt from the den as if shot. Jayne was looking upwards, mouth open, stunned. The nearby trees were thick with monkey-people, two of whom were climbing down with dangerous urgency.

Should they run? Jayne didn't think so. Running was an admission of guilt. Better to face them down, placate them if possible.

Hopes of entente, however, were short-lived. The two greasers barrelled towards Scott, the first shoving him in the chest almost hard enough to knock him over. Both men stank of drink and wore expressions of callous disgust. One displayed a swastika on his arm, the other on his necklace. They were not like the greeboes who hung round the *Royal George*.

Scott, however, stood his ground. As was his wont, he had rehearsed many worst case scenarios that afternoon, and since he had neither been stabbed nor shot he was remarkably equanimous. In Scott's world, a world of vivid imagination, anticipation was invariably worse than reality, even a reality as ugly as the swastika boys.

"What's the game, pal?" pressed the first greaser, whose blonde curls and general air of disdain could have made him Roger Daltrey's brother.

Scott did not reply. He breathed slowly and laboriously as if a concrete weight were on his chest. But he kept his eyes fixed on his inquisitor.

"What you after, mate?" asked the second greaser, pressing in to the action. He wore small shades and a chinstrap beard.

It suddenly occurred to Scott that the two men knew who he was – that he had been a subject of their conversations, that he'd been built up as an enemy like the pigs, the security guards, the breadheads. Unable to challenge those greater forces, the greasers were spoiling for a fight with him.

Scott boiled with frustration and resentment: the commonsense option, to stay silent, had become unbearable. "I'm looking for my tape recorder" he pronounced.

"Don't know what you're on about, mate", replied Daltrey's brother, almost before Scott's words were out. If Scott pursued his case, violence was inevitable.

At this point, Jayne played her joker. "Hey, guys", she said, "we don't want any trouble". From her inside coat pocket she produced a magnificent spliff, which she brandished before the greasers' eyes. It was like raw liver to a pair of cats.

"It's good shit" she said.

The greasers were uncertain how to respond; Scott no less. It was not part of his plan to kowtow to the thieves who guarded his tape recorder, and he had not expected it to be part of Jayne's.

"Come, on, guys" pressed Jayne, "I've offering you some top shit here"

The greasers conferred. "Let's have it" counselled chinstrap man.

Daltrey's brother considered. "He's staying here" he demanded, indicating Scott.

"No problem" replied Jayne.

Chinstrap man took the proferred joint, produced a lighter from his pocket, lit up and drew deep. "Fuck me!" he cried, exhaling in a fit of violent coughs, staggering slightly, then winking lewdly at Jayne. "Fuck...me" he repeated, then took another draw, after which Daltrey's brother relieved him of the joint and he sank into a sitting position.

Daltrey's brother handled the dope rather better, letting out a "wee-hoo!" then turning his close attention to Scott's face.

"Check to see that no-one is escaping" he intoned, "from Desolation Row"

Scott considered quoting the next verse, with its implied reference to Southampton, but thought better of it. After two more tokes Daltrey's brother's attention was focussed more on his own balance. Suddenly, to Scott's amazement, Jayne put both hands to his chest and gave him an almighty shove, sending him crashing backwards to the ground.

"Get it, Scott!" she yelled.

Scott stood motionless.

"Get it!" repeated Jayne, urgently flailing in the direction of the hovel.

Belatedly, Scott came to life, a very frenzied life, rushing into the hovel and strewing its contents wildly until finally catching a glimpse of silver, seizing his treasure and crashing back out, to find Jayne dancing side-to-side like a boxer over a stricken opponent. Chinstrap man was struggling to his feet, only to tumble back down with the help of another decisive shove from Jayne.

"Jayne!" cried Scott.

The two fled, haring round the perimeter fence in the direction of the stage, hardly aware of where they were going, so long as it was away from the enemy. *Delta Lady* thundered out from the PA, a victory anthem, though hardly a victory to be savoured with no obvious sanctuary in sight.

Jayne, unlike Scott a novice at cross-country, cried out for a breather. Scott feared the consequences as Jayne sank to her haunches, but Jayne was grinning gleefully. "F.A.B., Parker" she gasped, in between grateful draughts of air.

"Let's keep moving" urged Scott.

"Relax" replied Jayne, regaining her breath. "They won't catch us"

"How do you know?" asked Scott.

"Cut that joint with a mandy" replied Jayne.

Scott nodded knowledgeably. "Good move, Jayne" he said. The compliment was intended to restore a little authority, but she barely seemed to heed it.

"How's the tape?" asked Jayne.

Scott focussed on his recovered property. Nothing looked different about the Phillips EL3302, yet it seemed indelibly tainted by the alien hands it had fallen into. Scott checked the rewind, the play, and briefly the record.

"Seems ok" he replied.

"Cool" said Jayne. "Now all we need is Dylan"

Scott looked ahead. "I think you can get backstage this way" replied Scott, vaguely remembering Croker's site map and a rumour that Dylan had been smuggled in through a backstage gate to the west of the stage.

"You reckon we can get backstage?" queried Jayne.

"I've got a pass" replied Scott.

Jayne's natural cynicism was outweighed by the magic of the moment. They were on a roll, the night was buzzing with possibilities, and the chance, however small, of getting backstage with Dylan was irresistible. They pressed on up the path, guided by the perimeter fence till the path was just grassland, then a copse, at which point the fence turned sharp right in the direction of the stage.

Scott's memory was clearly wrong. There was no entrance to the west of the backstage area, merely a dense wood skirted by an older fence, a high wire one. The only possibility was to circumnavigate the entire backstage area through the woods in order to reach the entrance on the other side.

Jayne did not show great interest in the fate of the red squirrel, Scott's chosen subject of conversation as the undergrowth crunched beneath their hastening feet. But Scott's sudden concern for the little rodent, and the importance of the island to its survival, masked his growing anxiety: if he failed to make good his blithe promise that he could get Jayne backstage, the disappointment would surely wreck their momentum, and with it any chance of intimacy.

Like Dylan, he had to deliver.

Emerging back onto the dirt track that skirted the eastern side of the festival site, Scott's hopes took a nosedive. Yes, there was a gate up ahead, but closed and locked. Hardly surprising, perhaps, with the world's most famous singer-songwriter about to take the stage, but to Scott's mind at that moment yet another grim reminder of the new elitism being ushered in by Britain's first great pop festival.

Now doubly determined, Scott peered through the gap between the gates, spied a security guard and called for his attention.

"Got to get to the electrical compound" he declared, flourishing his backstage pass.

"No-one's coming in here" replied the guard. He was a small man with a broad Hampshire accent, looking slightly absurd in his overblown cap and uniform.

"It's an emergency" replied Scott. "We need fuses"

The guard shook his head.

"It's a fucking emergency!" cried Scott, with a sudden intensity which shocked himself almost as much as his interlocutor.

"Lights have gone in the toilet tent" added Jayne, unbidden, but welcome all the same.

"It's going to be fucking armageddon" continued Scott, quickly responding to Jayne's improvisation.

"Don't you carry fuses?" enquired the guard. He did not seem intellectually confident.

"Not these ones" replied Scott, sharply. "They're waterproof. They go under the ground, covered in monkey shit"

The guard chuckled mechanically.

"It's a waterproof compound!" Scott informed him, witheringly.

There was a pause, then the guard shook his head again. "No-one's coming in here" he repeated.

"Ok" said Scott. "Then you're going to take the rap for this. The press are crawling all over this site. Fucking Woodnutt's looking for any excuse to close it down. If people are wading in shit in the dark, there's going to be fucking dysentery and it'll be the last festival Fiery Creations ever hold"

The urgency of Scott's speech, reminiscent of the bad tidings he once delivered in an Isaac Watts production of the *Royal Hunt of the Sun,* clearly rattled the man on the other side of the gate. Press hounding had created a palpable air of backstage paranoia.

"I'll talk to the boss" he declared.

The guard retreated, Jayne squeezed Scott's hand, then through the narrow gap Scott espied Ray Foulk, white-suited, looking like an anxious version of Ray Davies on hunger strike. His conversation with the guard was brief. To Scott's delight, the guard came back and opened the gate.

"You can go to your compound" he barked. "Nowhere else"

Scott moved through, but the guard stopped Jayne. "You got a pass?" he ordered.

Jayne, to Scott's astonishment, flourished a backstage pass remarkably like his own. Admitted to the forbidden city, they hurried over the grass, past the press tent and behind the stage, giggling like children.

"How did you get that pass?" asked Scott.

"I took it out your pocket" replied Jayne.

Scott was delighted. "You're a crim" he said.

"Needs must" replied Jayne.

The pair arrived at the electrical compound, which abutted the west side of the stage. Not far ahead of them was a silver caravan.

"That's Dylan's caravan" remarked Scott: Matt had told him that. Croker's daughter had apparently had a nap in there, and not been too impressed. Very plain, she'd said. Better ones at Puckpool.

"Do you think he's in there now?" asked Jayne, excitedly.

"Probably" replied Scott.

"Shall we knock?" suggested Jayne.

"He might be sleeping" said Scott.

"Or shitting himself" suggested Jayne.

"Or both" replied Scott. They both laughed. Suddenly, Scott marched determinedly towards the caravan, then just as suddenly turned on his heel, marched back to Jayne and produced a small key. "Got to get those fuses" he said. With that he unlocked the padlock on the plywood door to the compound, and they entered that small and secret garden.

FOURTEEN

The electrical compound was most happily situated for the music fan. With the aid of the stepladder fortuitously placed beside the looms of cable, reels of catenary wire and flourescent boxes, it was possible to look over the edge of the stage, past the mighty Wem speakers to the performance area, where roadies were busily changing the common-or-garden mikes for state-of-the-art alternatives. The patience of the crowd was clearly wearing thin: the VIP area, from the sound of things, had become more of a VIP bearpit, even less civilized than those greasers in their hovel.

Scott's attention did not dwell long on these things, however. He had noticed something incongruous sitting amongst the boxes of plugs, sockets and spotlights: an acoustic guitar.

"That's Dylan's guitar!" he announced, opportunistically.

"How do you know?" asked Jayne.

"It's a…" Scott scrutinised the name on the headstock, "…Epiphone".

"A Epiphone?" repeated Jayne.

"Yes, a Epiphone" replied Scott, sensing correctly that he'd been rumbled.

"Give us a tune then, Scott" requested Jayne. She sat on a box, expectantly, and Scott felt the full weight of that expectation. He considered playing *Something In The Air* again, but that would make him seem predictable, and beside, he needed something which would address her, feel personal, draw her towards him.

Scott hurriedly processed his repertoire of love songs. It was not large. Love songs had generally seemed irrelevant and tawdry in the quest for the great and meaningful musical statements to which Butterhorn aspired. There was *Wichita Lineman*, which was quite haunting for a commercial pop song, but Scott always fucked up on the high note. There was *Hey Jude*, which had some credibility, but was full of all kinds of weird chords. There was *Honey*, that all-time classic by Bobby Goldsboro, but what if Jayne didn't get the joke?

Wait. There was a song tucked away in the back of Scott's mind, a love song, one which Gerry had recommended, in his usual cynical fashion, for softening up girls. It was *Reason To Believe*. Scott couldn't remember who wrote it, but the song had simple chords, a pleasant tune and an easy sincerity. Scott began to strum the chords, barely audible against the sound system pumping out over the field behind him. Jayne moved her box closer. Heart filling with inspiration, Scott sang, closing his eyes as was his habit. At the first chorus, he risked a glance at Jayne, to see her face most wondrously open and responsive. He remembered Jayne's advice not to frown as he sang, and threw on an exaggerated smile which won an equally exaggerated response, Jayne's eyes crinkling into crescents of delight.

Reason To Believe had been a great choice, not only because of its impelling lyric and lovely melody, but also because it was so short its impact had no chance to wane. As Scott strummed the final chord with a resonant flourish, Jayne gave a polite round of applause, then, with a little jerk of her chin, beckoned him towards her.

Scott lay down the guitar and leaned forward. Jayne took him gently round the back of the neck and rewarded him with a deep, luxurious kiss which instantly transformed Scott's previously inert member into a full-blown lovestick. When they finally broke from the kiss he was completely disarmed: he had to confess his love.

"I've never met any girl like you" he said.

Jayne's face became serious. "Scott" she began, "there's something I've got to tell you"

A mighty dread seized Scott. "What?" he asked.

"I'm not a girl, Scott" replied Jayne.

Scott's world stopped.

"I'm not a girl" repeated Jayne.

"In what sense?" warbled Scott.

"In the sense" replied Jayne, "that I am a twenty-one year old woman"

Scott breathed again. He was more than happy to accept that Jayne was a woman. Yes, joy of joys, a woman, and one willing to kiss a boy!

"Sorry" he enunciated.

"Don't forget it" warned Jayne.

"I won't" replied Scott.

Was more love on offer? Scott's driver was still in pole position, but the answer would have to wait, because at that moment a vast roar from the crowd signalled that something was happening onstage.

"Dylan!" cried Jayne.

Scott and Jayne joyfully wrestled for the right to climb the stepladder first.

"Tape recorder!" cried Jayne.

Scott had left the EL3302 by the guitar. Dashing to retrieve it, he returned to a view of Jayne's heels. Next second, the air was filled with a most wondrously loose and rhythmic country rock - but that famous nasal voice was absent.

"It's just The Band" announced Jayne, though the 'just' was singly inappropriate. The Band sounded like no other group on Earth, freely swapping vocals over keyboard and guitar licks as sweet as Southern Comfort. This was big music for a big night, and the yells for Bob were soon silenced.

Scott began to climb the ladder behind Jayne, but as he did so became aware that someone was thumping the compound door against the boxes of sockets they had hastily placed in its way.

The door was forced open far enough to admit a head, and that head belonged to Lewis Croker.

"What the fuck are you doing here?" he barked. Despite the Band's best efforts, it was loud enough to turn Jayne's head.

Scott quickly weighed up the situation: negotiation impossible; expulsion inevitable; flight imperative. For a split second he considered fleeing onto the stage, but that would be straight into the arms of security. There remained just one possible exit, and regardless of the consequences, Scott took it, Jayne instantly following.

Scott and Jayne had entered a subterranean world of scaffolding and wood. Though the light was dim and the ceiling low, it was just possible to stand upright and see the way forward, though Scott was more interested for the moment in looking backward, expecting to see Lewis's muscular form framed in the makeshift doorway through which they had escaped. As luck would have it, however, Lewis was not attempting to follow. The opening of the door in the side of the stage was strictly banned lest the light be seen by press hounds seeking a way backstage.

Every aspect of the Band's masterful musicianship was amplified in Scott and Jayne's magic cavern: the thumping union of bass and drums, the orchestral swirl of the Leslie, the joyful duel of piano and guitar.

"It's my dream!" exclaimed Jayne, with a gleeful grin. "I'm under Rick Danko"

Scott bridled. "He's not that good-looking" he replied.

"Oh shut up, Scott, he's beautiful!" countered Jayne. "Stop being so competitive"

Confident they were safe and alone, Jayne sank to her knees, tipped back her head and savoured her good fortune. Inevitably she had a little something prepared for such a situation.

"Fancy a J, Scott?" she asked, flourishing a spliff every bit as well constructed as the stage above.

"Is it cut with a mandy?" asked Scott.

"Don't worry, babe" replied Jayne. "I don't want to cripple you".

Scott was hugely pleased. No girl or woman had ever called him 'babe'. It was as if they were already a couple.

Jayne lit up, drew deep, then exhaled upwards past her nose. "Good shit" she murmured, and as if in reply, Rick Danko's soulful waver announced the beginning of *Long Black Veil*, a meandering country tale perfectly suited to the absorption of the sacred weed.

Scott took his turn with the joint. As ever, the tobacco made his head swim, but once the initial surge had died down, he was filled with euphoria. This was it, the night he'd anticipated for months, spent with a woman he could never have imagined, in the very guts of the festival. The future suddenly seemed full of possibilities.

"This is the best music I've ever heard" he declared.

"I told you it was good shit" quipped Jayne.

"No, seriously, it's not just the pot" replied Scott.

"The *pot*" mimicked Jayne. It was the word they used on the news.

"What?" complained Scott.

"Are you on the pot, Scott?" joked Jayne, in an officer accent.

"It's a good idea" mumbled Scott.

"What is?" asked Jayne.

"To be on the pot" replied Scott, "if you're having good shit" He collapsed into giggles, which rapidly infected Jayne, not that she found the joke funny. What was funny was the fact that Scott had said it.

"It's not really *progressive*" Scott suddenly opined.

"What, having a shit?" laughed Jayne.

"This music" replied Scott, refusing to take the bait. "It's traditional, but it's...modern"

"Like you, Scott" said Jayne.

"I'm not traditional" complained Scott.

"Oh, Scott" replied Jayne. "If only you could see yourself"

"I'm not!" protested Scott. "I go to a traditional school, and I hate it!"

Jayne viewed the hurt on Scott's face and her desire to tease evaporated. Scott was also better looking than he realised. "You'd better switch on your tape recorder" she advised.

"I'll wait for Dylan" replied Scott.

"You'll forget" said Jayne.

There was a pause.

"Forget what?" asked Scott.

"Switch it on, Scott" said Jayne.

Scott complied, though the task had become strangely onerous due to the immense difficulty in coordinating the three-way transport switch with the record button. Jayne watched his frowning struggle and eventual satisfaction with an indulgent smile.

"What?" said Scott, becoming aware of her expression.

"Come here now" said Jayne.

Scott shuffled closer. They kissed again, this time more urgently. When their lips eventually parted Jayne's mind was clearly set. "Any history of heart trouble?" she asked.

Scott's heart duly thumped. "Not till now" he replied.

"Get your kecks off then" said Jayne.

Scott hesitated. "Are you prepared?" he asked.

"I'm not stupid" replied Jayne.

Scott began to undress, Jayne too. There was little ceremony about it, almost as if they were undressing for badminton, apart from the state of Scott's shuttlecock. Yes, Jayne was undeniably female, her breasts emphatic if slightly pendulous, her hips wide, her underarms and thatch dark and untamed. Above such a glut of womanliness, Jayne's boyish trim was all the more piquant, and as the couple enfolded a musky, almost rubbery scent arose from her, more seductive than Shalimar.

Scott had first learnt the facts of life from a *Which?* contraception supplement; how miraculously now those diagrams came to life, how miraculously everything worked as it should, although no diagram had showed the woman steering the man into the right position, nor conveyed the luxury of concupiscent flesh. With insistent glorious motion they affirmed and reaffirmed their need for one another, as *Long Black Veil* gave way to *Kingdom*

Come, and *Kingdom Come* to *Ain't No More Cane.*
Surely they were at the very centre of the Earth, but even
here Scott maintained an islander's reserve, till Jayne
cranked his head so he was finally looking into her eyes.

Too beautiful.

"Can't stop" gasped Scott.

"I'll kill you if you come" warned Jayne.

Scott's mind urgently processed the anti-list to that of his
previous encounter with Wendy. Wendy herself…Orations
and Declarations…Founders and Benefactors…Double
Your Money… festival toilets…Alvin Lee guitar solo…

Jayne meanwhile had her own ideas, wrestling Scott
onto his back and taking up centre stage, where the show
could better be managed. Her raking talons delayed
Scott's little death far better than thoughts of Hughie
Green, but the beautiful urge still came to him prior to
her, followed by a supersensitive agony as Jayne reached
her own juddering conclusion. Finally she rolled off his
grateful sweating body to flop back onto the sun-starved
grass, better to comtemplate the profundity of the
sounds above. In wordless union the couple savoured *I
Shall Be Released* and *The Weight,* filled with the most
exquisite optimism, like a distillation of all the hope in
that blessed field.

Scott stroked Jayne's shoulder, then let his fingers run
down her gently muscled arm to her hand. She squeezed
his fingers, then held on. The Band broke into *Loving
You Made My Life Sweeter Than Ever.* Until that
moment Scott had pigeonholed Motown alongside all
the commercial nonsense Butterhorn were pledged to
supercede. He would never think like that again.

"Let's go on holiday" he said suddenly.

"We are on holiday" replied Jayne.

"Abroad, I mean" said Scott, warming to his idea. "Florence"

"You don't want to go there" replied Jayne.

"Why not?" asked Scott. "It's the most beautiful city in the world". He had seen a documentary about Tuscany on BBC2.

"It's a miserable place" replied Jayne, "like Doncaster"

"Have you been there?" asked Scott, deflated.

Jayne chuckled.

"I'm serious, Jayne" said Scott. "We'd have a brilliant time"

"You're forgetting something, Scott" replied Jayne.

"What's that?" asked Scott.

"Money" replied Jayne.

"I'd busk" said Scott.

"Oh yeah" replied Jayne.

"Seriously!" said Scott.

Jayne sensed Scott's vulnerability, felt for him, and abandoned her levity. "It's not going to happen, Scott" she said, as gently as The Band's volume allowed.

"Why not?" pleaded Scott.

"I don't do the couple thing, remember?" replied Jayne.

Scott's high dissipated. He withdrew his fingers. "Not even with Dave?" he grunted.

"Dave's my friend" replied Jayne.

There was a long pause.

"Do you sleep with him?" asked Scott.

"Sometimes" replied Jayne.

Scott rolled away into a foetal position.

"Come on" said Jayne, laying a hand on Scott's side which Scott abruptly removed.

"I don't want to get the pox, thank you!" he snapped.

"Everyone in the squat is checked for VD" replied Jayne.

"What, so you can sleep with all of them?" sneered Scott.

"If it makes you happy to think so" replied Jayne.

"No, it doesn't make me fucking happy!" snapped Scott. "You don't just sleep with people because they're you're friends!"

"What, is it better to sleep with people you can't stand?" retorted Jayne. "Like Cressida?"

"I never slept with Cressida!" protested Scott.

"Or Wendy?" continued Jayne.

"I never slept with Wendy!" cried Scott.

"And nothing went on between you" pressed Jayne.

"I never slept with her" protested Scott.

Jayne levelled an admonishing finger. "Before you criticise me" she pronounced, "you should look at yourself"

There was a long silence.

"Don't go back to the squat" pleaded Scott.

"It's where I live" replied Jayne.

"Live with me" pleaded Scott.

"Scott" asserted Jayne. "Try to understand. I don't do that. The way I live is the way I want to live"

"Degenerate crap" sneered Scott.

"That's what all the conservatives say" replied Jayne.

Scott leapt to his feet, hardly reacting as the top of his head smashed against the underside of the stage. "I am not a fucking conservative!" he yelled, and as if in response a hundred and fifty thousand people yelled their appreciation. The Band's set was over, but Scott's performance was just beginning. Leaving his scattered clothes, oblivious to Jayne's entreaties, he marched to the exit door and flung it open.

"I'm not a fucking conservative!" he yelled again, and this time his audience was a gobsmacked Lewis, who summarily abandoned his desire to bring Scott to justice, backing away to allow his naked adversary clear passage. Scott duly passed him and exited the electrical compound. How strange it was to strip away all defences and become so powerful.

So, where now? Like the students at the Sorbonne, Scott had made a radical commitment, but one lacking a chosen destination. He felt eminently human, yet as lost as a creature from another planet.

The next being Scott encountered wore the studded waistcoat of a roadie. He looked like he'd seen a few things in his time but the sight of Scott still left him nonplussed. "I'm an electrician" explained Scott, and as he said the word it took on a new meaning relating to the electricity within him, as if sex with Jayne was a kind of nuclear fission, unleashing energies which might feed the world or destroy everything.

Electric Scott capriciously turned away from the backstage area and into the nearest marquee. He had hoped this might be the press tent, but instead found a world abandoned by humans in favour of yogurts, crates upon crates of the stuff, every flavour from mandarin to raspberry to prune. Scott suddenly felt ravenously hungry. Without inhibition he began emptying the pots down his throat, their glutenous sickly sweet contents sliding down like slurry, pasting his mouth and spattering his ribs.

Was this theft? No. Scott was hungry, food was going to waste. It was social convention which stood in the way of morality, and that had been abandoned with Scott's jeans and pants.

Bourgeois justice, however, was not long in coming. The first security guard beat a hasty retreat, but soon returned with a further uniformed goon, advancing on Scott with clear intent of forcible arrest. Scott, however, had spent many hours shivering on the wing in house rugby matches, and was well-practised in avoiding the tackles of brutish props, even if this meant horizontal or indeed backward movement. Scattering yogurt pots in his wake, he dodged between the stacks of cartons and the tressel tables, escaping the tent and setting off on a mazy dash around two more, initially with no plan other than to run, then realising he must get back to Jayne, force her to witness him like Christ in Gethsemane, an image of fearless commitment pursued by the guardians of darkness.

And then Scott saw him: behind the stage, alone amongst a group of urgent debaters, nervously strumming. But oh no! What a dismally conventional figure he cut, white besuited, round-shouldered and meek, hair and beard neatly trimmed. They had got to him, the critics, the conservatives – they had scared him into submission. If only Scott could reach him now, seize his hand, bestow electricity...

"Bob!" Scott yelled. There was no response. Had he not been so stoned, Scott might have remembered that Dylan spent his entire life avoiding monomaniacs, nutters, stalkers and leftist missionaries anxious to reawaken the prophet within him. As always, the great singer kept his head down, lost to himself, utterly focussed on the trial ahead.

Undeterred, Scott hared towards the main man, desperate to make contact. Now, in the eyes of all who saw him, he was unquestionably a terrorist, one to be stopped at all costs. Ten yards short of his target, he crashed to the ground courtesy of a tackle from the side, executed by a besuited opponent he never saw coming, followed like a heavy rain by two, three more bodies, their rough boots and belts gouging into his suddenly vulnerable skin.

Minutes later, the arena erupted into an apocalyptic roar. But for Scott, the 1969 Isle of Wight Festival of Music was over.

FIFTEEN

The flying boats had gone, Calshot Spit lightship as well. The Hythe ferry still dodged the liners, but these now rose up even higher than the QE2, multiple decks like wedding cakes, dwarfed only by the blind hulks of the car transporters, daunting, ugly, strangely unfinished, like the brutal business of capitalism.

The Isle of Wight, thankfully, remained at the other end of Southampton Water. Red Funnel steamers still worked their relentless shifts from the Town Quay, but the yards that built the *Osborne Castle,* having been nationalised and re-privatised, were no more. The ferry Scott boarded had been refitted in Gdansk and painted in the national colours of Sweden, all the better to advertise that nation's flatpack flagship. The vessel was an ugly sight in Scott's eyes, but ironically he had just bought a kitchen from Ikea, seduced by the build quality and drawer dividers, enough to turn a blind eye to the founder's nazi origins and tax avoidance strategies. To compromise was human, but to rebel by walking in the opposite direction to the one-way arrows really was quite sad. But then Scott was sad, sad in every sense, and never more depressed than when spending lost afternoons in gargantuan department stores.

Scott's depression predated the news about Jayne, but that news seemed to crystallise all the deep dissatisfactions which underlay his increasingly comfortable life. He feared the journey he now undertook just as much as he looked forward to the journey of 1969. Back then he had welcomed destabilisation. Now it seemed he had a lot more to lose.

The site was not hard to find. Palmers Road had gained many new houses since the sixties, but beyond these the street miraculously reverted to the same dirt path a hundred thousand ragged souls had once tramped. At its conclusion, where Scott had once argued with nuns, a few senior citizens picked blackberries alongside the sacred field which had hosted the mother of British festivals. Far off to the west, Queen Victoria's deathbed still filled tourists with morbid curiosity. Ahead, over the Solent, the Spinnaker Tower marked Portsmouth's renaissance as a warfaring city. To the east was the path which had once led past the ill-fated disco tent, and wandering down this, the man Scott had come to see.

Owen's handshake was firm, accompanied by a manly squeeze of Scott's shoulder. He was a big man, several inches taller than Scott, with an imposing mass of greying dreadlocks, yet Scott immediately sensed there was something a little slippery about him. Though his eyes were the same colour as his mother's, the deadly honesty was absent.

"Sad day" he said.

"Mm" agreed Scott. Though on the verge of old age, close encounters still made him self-conscious, and given the significance of this particular encounter, he was reduced to looking at his shoes.

"It's good to meet you" said Owen, but even as he said it Scott sensed a trace of resentment, even hostility.

"I'm finding this very difficult" Scott admitted.

"Let's get it over with then" replied Owen. He fished into his rucksack and brought out a ceramic urn, slightly out of shape and decorated with a mosaic of small stones. "Hayley made it" he noted.

Scott nodded. His mouth was dry.

"How do you want to do this?" asked Owen.

"I don't know" replied Scott.

"I think we should climb over the fence" suggested Owen.

Scott acceded, sensing that Owen would have like to have climbed the fence whether it was necessary or not. Owen was an activist, a climate camp veteran, committed to the direct action tactics which had become increasingly fashionable since the defeat of the miners.

The two men climbed the fence, which wasn't high, and stood in the corner of the field, from which they would have once struggled to get more than a glimpse of Dylan.

"Do you want to say something?" asked Owen.

Scott's expression became weak and pained. He shook his head. Owen took the top off the urn and carefully scattered the contents over the grass. The fine dust was caught in a little gust of wind and a thin residue settled on Scott's shoes. It was the first contact he had had with Jayne since 1969.

Neither man cried: Scott because it was hard to cry over someone he had not seen for so long, Owen because he had stopped crying when Dave had left the Fruitland commune.

Owen again lay a hand on Scott's shoulder, but there was no reassurance in it. Scott wondered if this was an attempt to assert dominance: despite Owen's friendly words and actions, there was still a coldness in his eyes, and it would not have entirely surprised Scott if Owen had pulled a knife on him.

It could have been different. When Scott first learnt that the coil was not a failsafe means of contraception, he was prepared to give up his ambition to go to college, prepared (or so he thought) to take on parental responsibility, prepared for anything but to share Jayne's love. Though wilfully blind in so many ways, Scott knew he could not deal with the scenario she offered. That being the case, he could only cope by cutting himself off entirely.

Yet she remained always as a challenge to him, and in moments of weakness he would seek contact, if only by mail. Jayne always replied, sometimes curtly, but never withholding the information he sought. He knew how the squat had been terminated, and what efforts she had gone to to avoid the couple thing, the suburban thing, the atomisation, division and demoralisation which serves our masters so well. Along the way she had met the most appalling hypocrites, particularly those anti-authoritarian control freaks who seemed to be a feature of Jayne's every effort at communal living.

Near the end it was clear that all was not well in Jayne's head. It had become impossible for her to hold down a job; her last attempt, on the till of a Tesco Extra, lasted half a day. She had fought the law all her life, and in the end...you know the song.

"Jayne left something for you" said Owen. He reached again into his bag, and to Scott's astonishment produced a primitive cassette recorder. In the midst of the crisis all those years ago Jayne had mentioned it, but Scott had spurned anything that would remind him of the life he could never have. There had been the predictable row with Gerry, the final meeting between the pair, then the memory of the once cherished object had faded.

Owen bade Scott farewell, there was another handshake, then he was gone. It had been a remarkably unemotional meeting, deeply unsatisfactory, leaving Scott with a familiar feeling of incompletion. But solitude was welcome in that once overcrowded field. Expecting more frustration, Scott pressed the play button. To his surprise the little cogs turned and once more The Band worked their magic on Woodside Bay, though tinny, distant and much degenerated. Poor Rick Danko. Fought morphine addiction, died morbidly obese at 56. People said he was the nicest guy in rock.

Stepping away from the area where Owen had scattered Jayne's dust, Scott lay himself cautiously down. It was good to feel the grass and weeds around him. Such a shame that Dylan had entirely forgotten this place, if *Chronicles* was anything to go by. But then Dylan had made a career out of not giving people what they wanted, and the 1969 Isle of Wight Festival was typical in that respect.

Of course, there were thousands who would declare that it was a great gig, that it fulfilled their expectations entirely. But that depended on what those expectations were. Merely to be in the presence of celebrity was a fulfilment for many. *Self-Portrait*, however, the only album to feature live tracks from Woodside Bay, was widely derided as Dylan's worst.

For Scott, the performance he never witnessed was of little importance. It was just possible that Jayne had turned the tape over and recorded it, but Scott wasn't even inclined to find out. He had no desire to impress his old schoolmates now, there were bootlegs everywhere and you could even find a few videos on Youtube.

The recording to which he now listened, however, was unique. Not just unique because it featured the understage sound of The Band, but because Rick Danko was unknowingly serenading two young people fucking, and doing so with a gusto which was completely unremembered by Scott. Never had the urgency of life been more apparent, as Scott listened to the groans of the young Jayne as the dust of her bones lay on his shoe. Her reality came back as vivid as sunset, and with it the chaotic panoply of hope that underlay that ramshackle event on the Solent. Scott desperately wanted to tell her that he was still alive, that his own hope was still alive, and suddenly he wanted her every bit as ferociously as he had on that magic weekend. But she was gone, the army child, the nomad, no more. Scott pulled the rag from his pocket: now was the time for his tears. The relief was great, revelatory, and as his sobs subsided, Scott breathed deep of the island air. To his amazement, the magic was still there, like the boundless enthusiasm for music that still fired the star of '69, now 70 himself.

A new strength, wholly unexpected, filled Scott's tired heart. He had a new responsibility now, the responsibility to keep alive the spirit of Jayne: he would not let her down.

Lightning Source UK Ltd.
Milton Keynes UK
UKOW041653270513

211322UK00001B/65/P